For Cheryl
[handwritten signature]

Lifewheel

[handwritten: Kathy Kouzmanoff]

Your Choices at Life's Every Turn

- Needy Responder
- Successful Conformist
- Reflective Individualist
- Spiritually Mature Conscient

Kathy Kouzmanoff

"Kathy, this is excellent."

-Joseph Dispensa

"Easy to read, very insightful and helpful."

- Sr. Marion Abing

Printed in the United States of America.

Booklocker.com, Inc.
2007

Lifewheel

*Your Choices at
Life's Every Turn*

Kathy Kouzmanoff

To My Parents, For Their Love And Goodness

Raymond J Ritger 1922-2006
Rita Ann Schneider Ritger 1922-1990

Author's Acknowledgements

Grateful thanks are given to copy editors who worked on this book, Deborah Peterson and Robert M Wallace. Also heartfelt thanks to members of the Mind's Eye Institute, who began this project in a focus group on personal development. Finally, special thanks to students and readers who gave feedback on the manuscript as I wrote and taught it for ten years.

Table of Contents

Lifewheel: Your Choices at Life's Every Turn

Lifewheel Essentials
Your World of Integral Personal Development

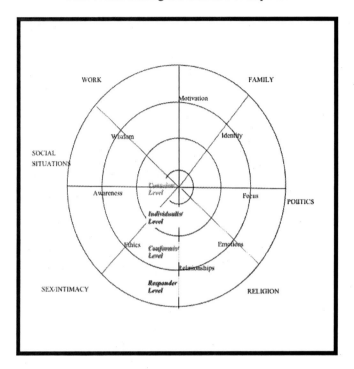

The Inner Lines of Your Personal Development

Motivation, Identity, Focus, Emotions, Relationships, Ethics, Awareness and Wisdom

The Outer Domains Of Your Social World

Family, Politics, Sex/Closeness, Religion/Arts, Social Situations and Work

Four Levels of Development

Responder, Conformist, Individualist and Conscient

Kathy Kouzmanoff

Balanced Growth[1]

Inner Personal	Outer Personal
Mind/Consciousness	*Body/Behavior*
Inner Social	Outer Social
Culture /Relationships	*Social Structure*

Dynamics Of Movement In The Spiral Of Life

Summary: You come into being, grow in doing & belonging, find complications, awaken to self- realization and then to interbeing.

Beginnings: Your core self arises out of timeless being, centering you, as it quickens your unique self and directs you throughout life's four stages.

Developing: You make progress from your needy and non-aware beginnings, happily developing and belonging, in both your inner and outer worlds, with change always present.

Finding Complications: You experience complications in yourself, with uneven development, imbalances, getting stuck, spiraling ahead and falling back. You find complications without: separation, differences, finding fault in others, and others finding fault in you. These complications prompt your receptive, reflective and more genuine self-awareness and self-actualization.

Living from Your Core Self: You learn to live more and more from your core self, more aware now of how things really are, within and without, yet remaining connected and harmonious, observing all, judging little, joyously living the paradoxes of Spirit in time.

Levels Of Personal Development

Level 1   **Responder**   **(Body)**
Needy, Naïve, Narcissistic and Non-Aware

Basic Task	Survive Physically and Emotionally
Basic Value	Neediness
Basic Belief	The World Is About Me.
Basic Problem	The World Is Not Just About Me.

Mottos: *It's My Way Or The Highway;* or *I'm Nothing Without You.*

Level 2   **Conformist**   **(Mind and Heart)**
Smart, Savvy, Sassy and Successful

Basic Task	To Take The Role of The Other
Basic Value	Doing And Belonging
Basic Belief	If I Am Good, Things Will Be OK.
Basic Problem	I'm Good But Things Are Not OK.

Mottos: *He Who Dies With The Most Toys Wins.* or *Love conquers all.*

Level 3   **Individualist**   **(Soul)**
Receptive, Reflective and Real

Basic Task	To Reflect And Get Real
Basic Value	Authenticity
Basic Belief	If I Am Myself, I Will Be Fulfilled.
Basic Problem	I Am Myself, But Something Is Missing.

Mottos: *I Gotta Be Me.* or *To thine own self be true, and thou canst not be false to any other.*

Kathy Kouzmanoff

Level 4	**Conscient**	**(Spirit)**
Conscious and Connected		

Basic Task   To Be Aware Of The Subtlety
And Interconnectedness of All Things

Basic Value   Being

Basic Belief   All Is As It Is.

Basic Problem   No Problem.

Mottos: *Sometimes I Sits & Thinks & Sometimes I Just Sits. or Love one another.*

Personality Type (MBTI)[2]
You are most energized by your favorite world, outer or inner, favoring either extravert or introvert. (E/I).
Type also influences how you take in things (S sensor/N intuitive), value (F feeling/T thinking) and organize your life (J judging/P perceiving), giving you a personality and spirituality style.

Personality Styles[3]
Traditionalists SJs; Experiencers SPs; Conceptualizers NTs; Idealists NFs

Spirituality Styles[4]
Unity NT; Devotion SF; Works ST; Harmony NF

Preface

Life is a circle.

We end where we began.

In the meantime we journey through the spiral of life.

Where are you in the spiral of life? Where are you on the journey?

How this Work Came to Be

Most of us live in multiple worlds, each with its own code for success. I know I have lived many lifestyles, going from farm family to convent to single young woman to inner city teacher to married suburban homeowner to Realtor to depth psychology to widow to step mom to mystical spirituality. They all have different rules for living. They all deeply contradict each other. There had to be a way to make order out of all of life's contradictions.

Lifewheel is an attempt to "bring it all together." It has been long in coming, over twenty years. It began naively enough, yet Lifewheel has led to a rich and elegant synthesis that may be helpful for seekers anywhere on how to live well in many worlds.

In the early 1980s, Carl Jung's work caught my attention. I had been introduced to Jung through the Centerpoint Program from Nashua, New Hampshire, being sponsored at the time by the Unitarian Church West in Brookfield, Wisconsin. I started picking up Jung's books as well, usually on clearance tables. Among those I collected was *Man in Search of a Soul*. He was hard to understand, but I liked him anyway! There was a sense of depth and meaning coming through that stirred my soul. Then I heard from my friend Karen Perkins that Jung had united the individual unconscious and its symbols with those common to all religions and philosophies. I was utterly intrigued, wondering how that could be, and what the content was. That motivated me to join the C G Jung Center in Milwaukee, where I eventually became vice-president. Early in 1985, I met a Jungian analyst Boris Matthews who was in training with the C G Jung Training Program for analysts in Evanston, Illinois and eventually taught there. I was eager to understand how Jungian insights applied to me as a woman, to marriage, feminine identity and career. I asked Boris if we could work together to explore these issues. He agreed and we met weekly for three years, working on far more than feminine issues. In fact, Boris wouldn't let me quit until the analysis was complete and I had brought together my outer and inner worlds into a whole, including universal symbols from other cultures that appeared in my dream and imagination life. Many of them I had never been consciously taught.

My inner life and I had formed a clear partnership. I learned what psyche wanted of me and I consciously submitted to its direction and its wisdom. So, initial curiosity and then commitment to what was asked of me from within, proved to be both empowering and exhausting. Marrying the conscious and the unconscious is still a source of dynamic living, both personally and professionally! In addition, I discovered, it is not without its dangers. I will say more about that later.

Through Jung's approach, I became immersed in the inner life for the second time in my life. I had been immersed once before, for nine years, in my adolescent and early adult years, while studying to be a Catholic nun, and taking first vows with the School Sisters of St Francis in Milwaukee. The approach in the convent now seems to create a contrast to Jung's. The Catholic world is highly institutional, emphasizing its founder, Jesus, the Bible and right doctrine for all, the hierarchy and the sacraments. For Jung, the inner life can be supported for some through religious institutions but his emphasis is on an individual's own inner spirit life, with its stream of symbols, dreams, body symptoms, work and relationship issues, fantasy and altered states of consciousness. They are then integrated into mature consciousness to achieve an enlivening wholeness called individuation.

My plunge into the inner life that began with analysis created a framework for deep exploration of the psyche that lasted for ten years. I would spend about three hours a day interpreting dreams, amplifying body perceptions and movements, taking fantasy and altered states of all kinds seriously. They were messengers from another deeper, wiser place in me and I journaled the conclusions. In addition I kept studying, always studying. There were times that I felt as at home in the inner world as I did in the physical world.

This inner work led to a powerful clearing of inner blockages and awakened the powerful kundalini energy asleep in each of us. It created a severe physical crisis as it rose up my spine and got stuck at my throat, causing palpable vibrations there, twisting my larynx from left to right and paralyzing my vocal cords. It lasted for months. The result was that I couldn't make a sound, not even a cry. An ear, nose and throat specialist said I looked like I had been hit hard from the side, which I had not. He had never seen anything like it, but said he would be thinking about it for a long time. Once my body had worked through the enhanced flow of energy, I could talk again and also began to see auras and anticipate people's ideas, all the while trying to fully integrate the increased energy flow into my all too culturally conditioned body. Sensitivity to myself and others was acute. I came to understand the subtlety and power of working with human energies and their powerful transformative effect on the body.

The involvement with the inner world proved to be a blessing and a source of strength when I most needed it. It provided a seamless transition when my husband John Kouzmanoff died in 1995. The love bond between us was decisively transformed from one of heart/body to heart/spirit, and it happened very naturally. We simply related heart to heart in this new way, with great joy!

Curiosity about how all forms of growth and success fit together was part of what drove me in my decade of study. It all seemed like a vast puzzle, the pieces of which had to fit together somehow. And slowly they did.

I revisited the current literature on career success. Much of it seemed to center on personal ego development and 'making it' in the world, and so had a markedly different focus from Jung's work of marrying ego and Self. I tried to unite career success with depth psychology. Doing so led me to rethink the content and structure of the adult education classes I was teaching at local colleges. I added layers of inner depth to the standard career development menu of personal interests, abilities and values, using fantasy in various forms to tease out more depth in students and then integrated both approaches for them.

However, it was Ken Wilber's many books, especially the earlier ones, which really made it possible for me to start putting together all the pieces of the larger puzzle.[5] What amazed me was that he had shown how every philosophy, psychology and religion contained a piece of the personal development puzzle. They all constituted a continuum. Even Jung, my most insightful teacher, was just one part of it!

Then, membership in The Association of Transpersonal Psychology led me to Dr. Roger Walsh's work. He held that all religious traditions contain basic principles that guide human development and that these need to be applied if one is to become spiritually mature. These principles found their place in the vast puzzle I was pondering, the puzzle of the many ways of knowing and living. *epistomology?*

All this was parallel with a continuing search for an open, yet integrative community, supporting personal growth. I talked with others and none of us could find it. I thought, in 1995, "Why not build it?" Therefore, with the help of numerous volunteers, The Mind's Eye Institute came into being, a non-profit organization aimed at doing just that. Its records are now archived with The State Historical Society of Wisconsin. It honored all growth traditions of the world: western, eastern, indigenous, psychosocial psychology, and holistic science. We developed courses on how we develop through stages, and on how the various aspects of our lives fit together. Margaret Roche, a member of the Institute, and I spent a full year leading a focus group based on Ken Wilber's *Eye of Spirit* to see what people wanted in a personal development organization. Then we devoted another year to designing the beginning framework of Lifewheel and taught it to the Institute's members.

Members of the focus group told us they wanted simple, accessible and yet insightful materials. They found Wilber took too much time to read and figure out. I decided to streamline what seemed to many, including varied professionals and professors, a very complex approach to integral development. I wanted to design something easy to read and easy to reference. I think I have done it in this work called Lifewheel.

Additionally, I was given some valuable advice in 1998 at the annual Association of Transpersonal Psychology's Conference in California, where I met Professor Peggy Ann Wright of Lesley College, Cambridge, MA. She advised that I include the insights from Jenny Wade's book, *Changes of Mind*. Wade knew about integrating the feminine into what was perceived as an overly masculine framework in most integral development. It seemed to me that she meant to add the 'affiliation mode' of belonging to the 'achievement mode' of developing. Basically, this means emphasize belonging as well as doing in the stages of development. I have tried to pay attention to both of these throughout Lifewheel.

Lifewheel is the end result of all these influences. I hope that Lifewheel is a user-friendly guide to integral development. Although it is not meant to be a scholarly work, it is based on extensive scholarship and mirrors the insights of scholars.

The Lifewheel image came from a dream I had in 1987.

Lifewheel is deliberately written very straightforwardly. In fact, it can be understood in just a few minutes, from the Reference Card Essentials and the Introduction. Lifewheel can be used by almost anyone open to universal truth underlying any growth tradition, in any culture or time or stage of development. Lifewheel attempts to offer inspiring and informative personal transformation basics.

Many believe that, as we develop ourselves, gaining personal wisdom and stability, we also contribute in some small way to the stability and transformation of our world. It reflects research on universal consciousness, in which we all participate. The 100th Monkey Syndrome is an example of such universal consciousness.

What is this syndrome? It refers to a study of one island of monkeys, who started to wash the sand off their food before they ate it. As more and more of them watched the others, they soon imitated this useful behavior. What was astonishing to the researchers watching this scenario over several years was that it started happening on another

island when the behavior had reached a critical mass on the first island. There was no physical connection between the two islands. What exactly happened here? Was there a sort of critical mass of consciousness change in the creatures, a critical mass that somehow jumped across the water? Was it the proverbial 100th monkey's changing his behavior that brought about the change in the species?

Finally, here is a great writer's story! I was doing Lifewheel workshops in San Miguel de Allende in Mexico and went into a small restaurant one night named "El Rinconcito" for a late night snack. This was a few days after all of my workshops were finished. There I met three women, two of whom I did not know, but one from Wisconsin whom I knew. None of them had taken part in the workshops, yet all of them were talking about Lifewheel! And, of course, they all claimed to be at the highest level of development, Level 4, that of the conscient.

This humored me indeed because, of course, we always want to think the best of ourselves. The joy of Lifewheel is that it loosens up the idea of what is natural and optimal. All levels of life are honored as natural. Spiraling in and out of levels occurs regularly, even daily, in our lives. It is our conscient core self with its mindfulness that can keep us centered and stable as we move through the spiral of life.

Lifewheel's 100 short chapters are easy to read, providing rich and elegant clarity. May your spirit soar, seeing your many-faceted life integrated in Lifewheel and your choices at life's every turn.

April 23, 2002; December 4, 2007

Lifewheel Introduction

You may be looking for balance in your life. You may need a system to sort out what to keep and throw and when. You may want to discern who makes a good life partner at 25 and who is good at 55. You may wonder how dreams fit in or how to order your sense of self. You may be looking for real unity in the world, versus adapting to the "real world." You may be looking to "bring it all together."

Choices in life are often contradictory and a system to sort out life's changing demands along the way could be helpful. A helpful system would compare the self-involved that isolates, the smart and savvy ways of success in the world, reflective and authentic self-expression, and finally, conscious and connected living of the unseen world in your daily life. Each would be given its rightful place.

These are a few of the things others have looked for, and found, in Lifewheel.

Lifewheel gives you an affirming bird's eye view of the pattern beneath the patterns of our daily lives. Lifewheel acts as a map on the journey of life, telling you where you are in the spiral of life. Lifewheel makes sense of the confusion that we are faced with every day, within and without. It helps anchor your own mindful living, giving you a framework for making informed choices.

1

Lifewheel is like standing in front of a hologram. If you visit the Museum of Holography in Chicago, you get to stand in front of a globe, seemingly lit from within, and you see figures within it, and they seem suspended in space, coming from seemingly nowhere. As you shift perspective, you see different things in the globe. It's just like the small hologram on the lower right corner of a Visa charge card, where the picture of a winged bird seems to move in flight, as you shift your perspective.

Lifewheel works like these hologram images. And so do we. We are like a hologram. Where we get our images of life from is ultimately delightful, and profound, to consider. What we see in life depends on the perspective we take on life. A shift in perspective changes our experience of being alive.

One perspective is based on a self-centered neediness: "It's all about me." In Lifewheel this is the responder stage. Some choices are based on success in the world, in both love and work. This is the conformist stage. Some choices are based on being true to yourself and what you deeply care about. This is the responsible, individualist level. Some choices are based on deep spiritual maturity and belong to the conscient level. Lifewheel provides four perspectives for you to consider, tracking inner and outer real-life issues level to level.

Here are some examples of how a life issue might shift level to level. You can see how choices might look from responder, to conformist, to individualist, to conscient.

EXAMPLES OF LEVELS IN PERSONAL DEVELOPMENT, INNER LIFE

<u>Detachment</u> goes from denial to a responder, to discipline for a conformist, to choice for an individualist, to freedom for a conscient.

<u>Independence</u> goes from willful rebel for a responder, to personally responsible group player for a conformist, to a self-reliant self-starter for an individualist, to an interdependent person as a conscient.

<u>Love</u> goes from enmeshment for the responder, to cooperation for the conformist, to respect for differences as an individualist, to <u>*All are one*</u> as a conscient. What means

<u>Perfection</u> goes from rigidity for the responder, to material appearances for the conformist, to uniqueness acknowledged for the individualist, to universal acceptance for the conscient.

<u>Personal Power</u> goes from control over others for the responder, to compromise for the conformist, to candid diplomacy for the individualist, to loving service for the conscient.

<u>Silence</u> goes from boring for the responder, to useful for the conformist, to essential for the individualist, to sacred for the conscient.

EXAMPLES OF LEVELS IN SOCIAL DEVELOPMENT, OUTER LIFE

<u>Personal Boundaries</u> go from blaming others for the responder, to healthy limits for the conformist, to conscious choice of roles

for the individualist, to strong and supportive of others for the conscient.

War Politics goes from unawareness for the responder, to cooperating with government for the conformist, to democratic debate for the individualist, to working for peace for the conscient.

Belief or Disbelief in God goes from rigid fundamentalism for the responder, to group norms for the conformist, to considered deliberation for the individualist, to respect for freedom of belief for all as a conscient.

Sex goes from satisfying drives for the responder, to social codes for the conformist, to honesty about its power for the individualist, to pleasure in giving and receiving for the conscient.

Neighbors go from behaviors of irritation or exploitation for the responder, to group give and take for the conformist, to honest relating for the individualist, to heartfelt interconnected flow for the conscient.

Job change goes from fear and isolation for the responder, to a "can do" attitude for the conformist, to self-actualizing opportunity for the individualist, to ongoing renewal for the conscient.

You might see that these stages of life become increasingly more subtle, insightful, demanding and fulfilling of your potential. You may be surprised at the demands of living one's highest potential. Yet, there it is, a path as perennial as life, a path made clear and simple for you in Lifewheel.

There is a truckload of scholarly research behind Lifewheel. And a lifetime of experience! You get it all distilled down to a few words per level. How's that for simple and easy to understand?! Lifewheel is written in disarmingly simple form, with short chapters and topics tracked at each level. This allows you to easily flip back and forth, as you compare and contrast how life looks at each level. Over and over I've seen people glance at the four levels summary in Lifewheel Essentials and "get it" instantly. Lifewheel is a sophisticated self-assessment tool and can provide extraordinary strength and clarity in one's mental health.

I have been on a personal development path since my dad put me on a tractor at age six to drive for the hay crews. It morphed into nine years in a convent, an utterly worldly life when I left the Franciscan order, later conventionally settling down into marriage and mortgage, and at age forty, stumbling onto the brilliance of the inner life, and learning to create a dynamic partnership with it. The journey to life's highest realizations now continues for me.

One of the reasons I left religious life, and still have trouble with any official creed, is that I see any single worldview as too small. The map is often confused for the destination and reflects the limits of the believer's personal experience. At the same time, I realize that once in my development I too thought I had "the" answers. I now realize that having "the" answer for others is entirely normal at a responder or conformist stage.

As farmer's daughter, nun, wife, teacher, sales woman, analysand and mature spiritual seeker, I have lived life from many perspectives, in systems that were sophisticated and demanding. But they contradicted each other. So, in a way, I wrote Lifewheel to make sense of the contradictions I experienced in my own life. Lifewheel has made order for me of many ways to do life. It helps me to make insightful choices, when I lose perspective. I now also see, from the conscient level, how life is paradox. Some choices are better than others, and yet, essential human dignity gives us all the right to our evolving place in the spiral of life.

LIFEWHEEL, PART ONE: DYNAMICS OF MOVEMENT IN THE SPIRAL OF LIFE

It's not pretty, or easy, for anyone to look at the unflattering sides of ourselves. However, there is a way to do it that eases the pain. Part 1 of Lifewheel brings this means into focus. It provides a gentle overview of the inner dynamics of your core Self, how it acts as a stable home base of unchanging strength for you and how it provides direction in the spiral of life.

You might find that, from your core Self, you can look at your more changeable self, explained in Part 2 of Lifewheel, with a certain dispassion, as if you were looking upon yourself on a movie screen. This observer Self is your timeless, original, deep and strong Self. Your core Self can see the complications of life and yet maintain equanimity. And your core Self always is always available to you, as a place from which to live with inner stability, awareness, openness and harmony.

It is hoped that from this secure place within your own being, you may find the sheer guts it takes to look at Part 2 of Lifewheel. Your desire to know yourself in your complexity, despite the challenges, is part of the Self's urging to know itself within you, in time.

You might consider your core Self as a life-long companion in the journey of life. It is the source of your beginnings. It impels your growth. It provides stability in the complexity of life. And finally, your core Self urges you to know Itself, create a partnership with it and live out of it consciously. Your source is also your goal.

LIFEWHEEL, PART 2: LEVELS OF DEVELOPMENT AND THEIR WORLDS

You have unlimited potential! Lifewheel focuses on just a few representative lines of this potential, in your inner and outer worlds. The inner life includes motivation, identity, focus, relationships, emotions, ethics, awareness and wisdom. These topics were chosen because they arise over and over in the literature as universal issues in personal growth.[6] The outer domains of family, politics, religion/arts, sex/closeness, social situations and work are found to be most common references by people to their social lives.[7]

Lifewheel gives you immediate insight and outlines the range of choices available to you wherever you are in the spiral of life. Each point is described in disarmingly simple terms. The chapters are short and on an easy reading level. Taken together, these options gradually reveal a landscape, or a hologram, if you will, of your life. Depending on how you look, on the perspective you take, just as looking into a hologram, you can see the part or the whole, or both, at once.

You can see yourself, others, how others see you from their place, where your society is and even where international world events are. All are clearly in their place, and it is easy to see why they clash or cooperate. Once you know the basic pattern, you can instinctively see how any point on Lifewheel relates to all the others. Lifewheel provides you a paradigm, a pattern of life's dynamics, providing heightened flexibility, to more effectively deal with contradictions and differences.

Enjoy seeing yourself on this wheel of life! You are human and rich with multi-layered experiences, many of them contradictory. You may find that this map of your life journey instinctively makes sense. Its wisdom is written deep in our hearts, even in the hearts of us moderns, whose lives are so cluttered. All the world's growth traditions, those of psychology, of religions and of holistic science are all reflected in Lifewheel.

We all start as responders and often revisit it, especially under stress. The observer in your core Self (Explained in Part 1) can help you deal with possible shame and denial, common to responder issues.

If you see yourself at the second stage (conformist), you may observe how common these traits are, and how culture spends lots of money and effort to keep us at this level.

Of course, many of us desire to identify with the higher stages of development, to think of ourselves as individualists, or as spiritually mature people, that is, conscients. Why not? We all have an instinctive sense of our highest and best selves, and may have already made significant progress toward these levels.

The reality is that all of us are on all four levels from time to time. Sometimes we are centered and whole. Sometimes we do well in one area and not another. And sometimes we spiral back and forth, progressing and regressing in sudden spurts and jumps. Even these complications are part of the richness of life.

You may notice, as you experience the four stages, that life is quite different at each of these vistas. It is as if you are seeing the world and doing the world in a whole new way at each level.

Your journey of personal development is relentless and lifelong. Much of it is not even your own doing. You are enlisted by your deepest Self to become your own hero/heroine in your life's adventure. Along the way there are gardens and deserts, enchantment and despair, reprieves and battles. You do not take this journey alone, whether you realize it or not. The world's diverse growth traditions are all around. And so is strength and renewal within from forces unseen. Lifewheel may assist you by mapping the way.

Lifewheel is simple, practical and dynamic in its design. It has subtle and alluring beauty, affirming the core goodness of the complex and awesome journey of humans in time.

WHO CAN BENEFIT FROM STUDYING LIFEWHEEL

In General
- those seeking a framework for development of persons and cultures in the spiral of life
- those living with the paradox of respecting development, while holding to a natural hierarchy of values
- those who desire the exhilaration of integrating body, mind, heart, soul and spirit

9

Individuals
- seeking a framework making sense of human contradictions
- seeking choices available in daily life events

Work Places seeking direction in
- supporting diversity
- enhancing personal growth
- enhancing higher values

Families in need of a roadmap
- for raising children
- for making choices about life direction

Churches looking to
- clarify the various stages of spiritual growth
- explore points of commonality with other religious traditions

Health Agencies
- promoting a holistic approach
- exploring the relationship of complementary care modalities to each other

Schools, book clubs and support circles seeking easy-to-use, rich material in
- self understanding
- social response

How to Use This Book

Lifewheel can serve as a quick reference handbook. It can show you where you are, where others are, and what choices are available to you at life's every turn. Let Lifewheel provide you with inspiration, insight and solace, wherever you are in the spiral of life. Most importantly, may it help you remember your original Self and its richness, as you travel along.

How Not to Use This Book

Lifewheel can assist you in exploring the underlying, universal patterns of personal and social growth. It not intended to make choices for you in personal, work-related, legal, moral, medical or spiritual matters. These decisions are yours to make, often with the help of other appropriate professionals, reflecting your own dignity, freedom and personal responsibility, which are key to the journey.

How To Use Lifewheel as a Personal Study Program

- Set aside time every day for regular study and personal growth practices.
- Create a Lifewheel Journal
  - o Record the date and chapter that you are reading.
  - o Identify a statement or main idea that is most striking to you.
  - o Ask yourself why the statement or idea is so striking and make notes for yourself.
  - o Consider a choice you are making from Lifewheel's four levels, noting the pros and cons of each, to help you make an informed decision.
  - o Draw conclusions and make a plan of action.
- Consider sharing your Lifewheel study with another individual or a group.
- Use Appendices in Lifewheel for additional help.

Lifewheel

There is a season for everything, a time for every purpose under heaven. Ecclesiastes 3:1

Part 1 Dynamics of Movement in the Spiral of Life

Beginnings from the Center

1 The Big Self, Capital "S"

You, my fellow soul traveler, are on a spirit journey in time. It doesn't matter whether you are aware of this or not. Unseen forces guide, direct, stir and distress you from birth to death. This partnership of you and spirit in time is the journey of your lifetime. Literally. Infinity strains to become actualized through you in time. You are a journey of timelessness in time.

You were born with many parts to your being. One is the big Self (with a capital "S"). It is your center, the part of you that is always you, that never changes, that continues the same from birth, through childhood and all your life. This big Self is sometimes called the true self or your center or your soul. It is often referred to as your inner life or Spirit and sometimes as your "unconscious" as well.

Whether this center is yours alone, or your connection to a universal quickening, or both, is wonderful to contemplate. If it is just yours alone, the big Self gives personal stability to your sense of self throughout your life. If the big Self is part of a grand universal ground of being in which you participate, it gives you insight and connection to all that is, far beyond what you could be expected to have as a separate individual.

2 The Little self, Small "s"

Another part of your being might be referred to as the little self, with a small "s." It is the part of you that changes throughout your life. Some call it your identity or your ego. It is who you think you are at any given time or place. It is the part of you that starts when you are born, and in some part, depending on your beliefs, dies with your body.

Part of the little self is the roles that you play in life. The roles are called the "persona" or the masks you put on. Your ego is usually bigger than your persona. It contains more sides of you than any given role that you play. One of the many other sides that a healthy ego can take in is one's weak or undesirable "shadow side." In this way, you acknowledge both your strengths and weaknesses. This requires a strong sense of self.

The little self or personal ego can be quite strong, and even must be, to deal with the tensions that come from holding together the differences between roles you play, the shadow side, and other powerful parts of your being. The little self usually grows in strength in the outer world as it matures. In the inner world the little self is most strengthened by its connection to the big Self.

3 The Seeker Within

There is within you a restlessness, to do more, to be more, to be somebody special, to understand how things are, a longing to be your true self. This longing is relentless, giving you peace only briefly, when you arrive at steps along the way, and then beginning again. This seeker within urges the things of a child when you are young, the gifts of love and achievement when you grow up, your unique self-actualization as you mature, and finally, awareness of Spirit. (which was actually with you all along the way).

There are many descriptions of this seeker within. Some writers liken your unfolding to the acorn becoming a mighty oak. Philosophers say that your growth and freedom is an infinite God expressing itself in finite time. The experience of the seeker within is often likened to a journey. Through its journey, the seeker usually comes to know much of the spiral of life very well, as it finds its own unique path.

The seeker within seems to be endlessly forging a partnership between your conscious, little self and newly emerging directives from the big Self. This cutting edge between what is and "what wants to happen" goes on in every present moment. This powerful unfolding, at the edge of what is and what wants to happen, naturally impels the seeker through the journey of life.

4 The Way

If life is a journey, you may wonder what map to use. In using any map, it is useful to keep in mind the wisdom of Taoism's Tao de Ching: A way can be a guide and have names, but it is not a fixed path with enduring fame.

Your personality, interests, abilities and values provide a natural direction. Beyond that, the world's five major growth traditions each have their own wisdom on the finer points of the path.

The first is the Judeo/Christian/Muslim tradition, all beginning in Judaism. The Old Testament writings, Abraham and Moses, begin the Jewish tradition. The Christian tradition follows the teachings of Jesus and the New Testament. The Muslim tradition is based on the Qur'an and Mohammed. In these traditions, the sacred writings, the founders, their immediate followers and the ongoing authority of the clergy are all important for the right way.

The Eastern traditions, such as the Hindu and Buddhist, are more focused on awareness within as the path to your full self-realization. They too have their teachers and varying traditions and strict disciplines.

The Indigenous teachings of Native peoples the world over emphasize connection to natural energies, of which you are a part. These are considered sacred, and used, for example, in contemporary Wicca practice.

The "psychosocial tradition" is a little over one hundred years old, sometimes using ancient stories called archetypes to better understand ongoing human patterns. It focuses on normal growth and its difficulties, often using the scientific method. Sociology, behaviorism, Freud, Jung and transpersonal psychology are a few of its many examples. Ken Wilber is associated with integral psychology.

"Holistic science" integrates approaches that represent body, mind and spirit. It may even go so far as to foster balance in one's inner and outer, personal and social lives, as Lifewheel does.

Some traditions insist that people should live by them alone. It seems that many people today use the traditions to richly marry wisdom and insight from several sources. It also seems that in times of social unrest, holding on to one tradition to the exclusion of others provides increased personal security.

Lifewheel is a universal pattern for all of the growth traditions, attempting to clarify the deeper unifying aspects they provide, as well as giving each their rightful place in the spiral of life.

5 Your Center Home Base

As you journey, you may find the need to stop and take a rest along the way. Your core self, the Self, your personal center, may be your most secure and permanent place of rest, renewal and freedom. It is your true self, wise and kind, full of connection and compassion for others and for yourself. It is content and always available to you. The beauty of temples and cathedrals remind us of this awesome space within.

When deep within your personal center, you know that your journeying in life is but a foray into time. It is a necessary journey. Sometimes it is a journey that seems complicated. The journey into time seems Janus-faced, sometimes alive with majesty and beauty, sometimes ugly and dark. But, from your core self, all of these experiences of daily life are buffered, as if you are in two worlds, one experiencing and one watching. The core self watches.

How to return home to your core self, your place of freedom, well-being, contentment, natural happiness and even bliss, has long challenged humanity. It is the central puzzle for every growth tradition. This home base of our core self is both the source and the goal of our journey in the spiral of life.

Making Tracks: Developing in Doing and Belonging

6 A Pyramid of Developing

One pattern in the spiral of life is development. In theory, it is a slow, steady and step-by-step moving up. You begin by satisfying basic needs for survival, maturing out of dependency and neediness, to developing your talents in work and love.

This growth may continue beyond the cultural norm of everyday expectations. It may continue into actualizing your own distinctive contributions. And it may go beyond even that, to full spiritual awakening.

The urge to grow is supported from within. Your potential, your best, is free, is yearning, has a passion, a vision, a quest, and urges you onward. This inner seeker is there from the beginning in you.

The support for your growth is outward as well. It's found in home, family and the larger community. School and church and the law and government all foster this growth. Sometimes you must seek out groups to take you beyond the norm.

Things can go wrong, inwardly and outwardly, in your growth. Inwardly you can become deeply confused, isolated, depressed and unable to thrive. Outwardly, you can lose motivation, get stuck in patterns of no growth or of alienation and destructiveness. You may find little social support, or only to a certain point. Only by admitting your pain and having hope of feeling alive again, will you have the urge to find a better way.

You are becoming more alive as you grow. For you are becoming more aware and more connected and more free. These inner qualities are part of the unseen reality that some call "spiritual," and they have been with you all along the path.

7 A Network of Belonging

Besides development in the spiral of life, there is the cultivation of heartfelt attachments, of belonging, of finding kinship. You might speak of this as creating soul, a capacity to feel deeply, to be moved, to care, to become attached. Developing your abilities can get you far in the world, but such concentration can also create a feeling of isolation or detachment from life. Doing is therefore beautifully balanced by belonging, that wide network of connection that plunges you deeply in life. There is nothing detached about belonging.

Modern culture very much works against deep attachment. We work too hard and too long. We move too much and ties get broken. Desiring ever more experience and development, takes the focus off of cultivating belonging. Economic independence isolates individuals. Yet, our souls yearn for community, the right place and the right people, where we belong.

Despite the challenges, kinship is where you find it. It may be family, friends, a neighborhood, a special interest group, co-workers and customers. Personal development groups, such as those found in the growth traditions, can also provide both belonging and developing, and so may be especially rewarding.

8 Going Inner

One world you move in is the inner world of self-consciousness and self-realization. All growth traditions emphasize this self-development. The most important elements of inner growth seem to be motivation, identity, focus, relationships, emotions, ethics, awareness and wisdom.[8]

Some people prefer the inner world to the outer world. They are called introverts. A natural introvert is actually someone who gets energized from within. The inner world is their favorite world. So they go naturally to read, to get lost in their projects, to create beauty or to explore other forms of self-expression and self-realization. They love being in nature. Socially, an introvert looks for sharing that is personal and has some depth. The inner world is favored by the personality styles of conceptualizers and idealists, and the spirituality styles of unity and harmony.[9]

"Going inner" can feel foreign if you aren't used to it, especially if you spend most of your time in the outer world. It may be the pain of the unfamiliar, the repressed, or simply lack of practice. Going inner is easier for an introvert than an extravert. The experience of going inner varies at the different levels of development as well. On the needy level it can feel like loneliness. On the developing levels it can feel like personal direction and even-temperedness. On the higher levels it provides opportunities for self-discovery, sweet solitude and naturally felt connections, sometimes all at the same time.

9 Going Outer

A second world you move in, besides the inner world, is the outer world. It is the realms of family, politics, religion, sex/intimacy, social situations and work.[10] Some say that these all boil down to love and work.

Natural extraverts get their energy from being in the outer world. They thrive on the people, the action, the sensory delights and adeptly being in the world. Extraversion favors the personality styles of traditionalists and experiencers and the spirituality styles of devotion and works.[11]

"Going outer" is natural, as we project ourselves, growing up, onto the world around us. It is a huge leap to withdraw the projections and see that how we see the world reveals aspects of ourselves. Projection also explains how, when we are in the higher stages of spirituality and identify with God, we come to see God and ourselves everywhere, and so experience unity everywhere as well.

Birth patterns encourage achievement in the first child, peacekeeping in the middle child, and a sense of entitlement in the youngest.   What you love in the outer world generates identification and attachment. Some would say that this is how you experience and develop your soul, your capacity to be moved, to feel, to become attached.   The outer world also can create addictions, if you rely for your well-being too much on anything outside of yourself, rather than your true, inner Self.

Going outer feels natural to the extravert. It feels foreign to the introvert, who favors the inner life. On the needy level, the extravert feels shy. On the developing levels the extravert is sociable, engaged in life and responsive. On the higher levels, extraversion is matured by connection to the Self, giving form to new ways of living, meeting creative challenges that unite inner and outer, personal and social. There are nurturing rituals, universal compassion, good works, love and freedom, often all at the same time.

10 Change

Change is the only constant in your outer life. Some change happens to you, while some you make happen. Certain changes can tell you where you are in the spiral of life.

Merely showing up for life brings change, personally and socially. You can encourage your own growth by the right attitudes: hope, honesty, humor, plans, patience, courage, determination, generosity and the intention to do your best every day. Don Juan, in Carlos Castaneda's writings, sums up doing your best by advising, "Be impeccable."

Changing poor or crippling patterns, whether from childhood, trauma or poor choices, requires living the right attitudes. Out of these right attitudes you can take one small step after another to a new thing, to overcoming your past, and so, get yourself free. Thus you learn to ride your own cutting edge, where change, the present moment ever rising and falling away, is both scary and exciting at the same time.

Different kinds of changes are called for at each level. Responder changes bring discipline to your out-of-control needs and impulses. Conformist changes build cooperative skills in work and love. Individualist change integrates what you want out of life with what life wants out of you! Conscient change demands regular practices, to hold you strong in your higher standards that are subtle, powerful, exhilarating, and unseen, flowing from within your spirit.

All change builds on the stages before it. Higher stages are by definition responsible, not self centered. Stages of growth nest, as the Russian matrioshka dolls nest, one fitting into another. A stage is higher if it integrates the skills of the previous stages.

Some things you can't change, such as other people. The Alcoholics Anonymous Serenity Prayer says it well: *Lord, give me the courage to change the things that can and ought to be changed, the serenity to accept the things that cannot be changed, and the wisdom to know the difference.*

Finding Complications on the Path

11 Many Places at Once

You may find that you react in contradictory ways to a given situation. It may seem confusing and stressful, for example, to think one way and feel another, and act even another. Coming from many places at once in the spiral of life is normal, and there is a reason for it.

You have an inner life and an outer life. You have many lines of development and different domains in which you live. You may be strong in one area and weak in another, needy in one, well adapted in another, and way beyond the norm in yet another. So, if you are that complex, and the people around you are too, how do we manage to keep it all together?

We can ignore or repress complications. We can follow the conditioned, social patterns to deal with differences. We can also strengthen our natural capacity to focus mindfully. Mindfulness is receptive awareness, a way of focus that takes things in, in complex, multilayered ways. It is open, receptive, yet stable and free, choosing to act or to let things be. Mindfulness integrates complexity into a personally pleasing, meaningful whole.[12]

As long as these social patterns and self-regulating behaviors keep the peace, it seems good enough. And for much of life, it works. However, when the tensions within you or between you and other people get to be too much, it may be a great relief to acknowledge the problems.

This tension of being in many places at once may also urge you to grow where you are weak, relying on where you are strong, in

23

order to relieve some of your strain of being in different places in the spiral of life.

Strengthening mindfulness is an excellent way of coping with complexity. Solitude, quiet and observing the many places you and others come from create a kind of distance and strengthen your sense of Self.

12 Balance and Imbalance

When your life is in balance, the inner and the outer, the personal and the social, you experience comfort in your body, contentment in your emotions, peace of mind within, and harmony in the world without. When your life gets out of balance, your body feels sick, your emotions are stressed, your mind is confused and you may be out of harmony with the world.

Your many worlds compete, the inner and outer, the personal and social. Your inner seeker, urging more development, or a consumer culture, generating restlessness, or your life falling apart through too many demands, change, loss, accident, illness or death, all these can create imbalance. You may not be able to access your core self, instead feeling overwhelmed when these all become too much. Things may be a mess in your life, as well, and you may not be able to maintain a graceful presence as you wobble to regain your balance. The resulting chaos isn't pretty, with your loss of Self showing. Your loss of Self shows in sickness, irritability, confusion, defensiveness, anxiety, depression and hopelessness. Faultfinding, addictive behavior or giving up may be tempting solutions.

To restore balance may take some time. You may need to rest, to be still, or be alone and mindfully deal with difficult emotions or relationships. You may need to then act courageously to re-establish balance. Ask friends, professionals and groups for help. Ask for what you need. Courage to change is important. Other people are important. And sometimes so is grace.

13 Getting Stuck

All the natural dynamics of movement in the spiral of life can come to a screeching halt. Developing, belonging, going inner, going outer, and working with change can all get stuck. Instead of a natural progression, you may seem to repeat the same old, tired, useless, neurotic patterns over and over again.

Stuck, neurotic behavior may make you seem difficult, unreliable or unstable in your day-to-day life. You wobble between this and that, but can't seem to make useful choices. Others may have little patience, getting frustrated at the helplessness of it all.

Serious trauma of some kind is often at the basis of such useless behavior and keeps you from growing. Unmet physical, emotional or social needs can all get you stuck. Try to understand and meet those needs. Unfortunately, these issues may be unconscious and you may have no idea why you keep making the same mistakes over and over. You must have the will to change and the courage. Looking to see where a pattern started can give you a clue, and this clue may be what you need, to break out of the repeat pattern that is keeping you stuck.

Changes needed vary from level to level in the spiral of life, as I mentioned earlier. As always, getting unstuck requires that you admit that there is a problem. It is often this personal pain that impels you to find relief, and the courage to get real about what's needed, and to get you free to move on in the spiral of life.

14 Spiraling Around

Under stress, loss, suffering, disillusionment, excessive demands or frustrations, you may find yourself spiraling backwards to needy behaviors or old habits of coping. These older habits of coping may not be as good as your more mature ones. For example, if you normally use spiritual practice to deal with problems, but now you are overwhelmed, you may become self-centered, irritable and finding fault with others and with the world. You may question your own self worth. Am I right or am I wrong? Am I good or am I bad? All of these are signs of stress and unhappiness and spiraling backwards.

You may sometimes also find yourself spiraling upward to sudden heights beyond your normal self. You may experience sudden insight into yourself or others. For the moment, you may become more tender, courageous or generous than is your norm. You may even be filled with gifts of Spirit, and be filled with joy and love beyond all logic.

Sometimes, if your little ego self is strong enough, you may want to deliberately spiral backwards, so that you can get insight into yourself, particularly into older patterns that seem to still cause difficulty for you. These new insights allow you to get beyond the stifling patterns, and you may be free to let them go, once they are conscious. This reflective look at yourself also lessens unconscious projections of your personally unacceptable shadow side onto others. This leads to less conflict with others, who no longer need to carry your projections for you.

27

The movement of your spirit spirals regularly. It is a very regular and normal part of your life. It is part of the richness and freedom and balancing of your magnificent Self in time.

15 Others Along the Way

Your overall character of regular patterns reflects your place in the spiral of life. From this place it is only natural that you see others from your vantage point. The same is true of every other person you encounter. They too have an overall character that gives them a place in the spiral of life and a certain point of view on you. So you may share their perspective on life, or it may be quite different.

If you share a similar place with others in the spiral of life, you get along, are bosom buddies or feel like soul mates. If you are at different places, you may find each other hard to understand and sometimes practically feel like you are from different planets. You literally see the world from different vantage points.

Individuals will respond to your growth differently, depending where they are in life. Those who are ahead of you will applaud your development. Those behind or near you may be upset, not knowing why you are changing, perhaps finding you uppity, too sensitive or a troublemaker. They may not know how to relate to you for a while. New patterns of understanding need to be established and this can take some time.

Our own need for self-protection makes us wary of people who are different from ourselves. We may instinctively protect ourselves by insisting on our rightness and their wrongness. As we mature, these defensive needs become more discriminating, seeing danger only where it really is, while letting others have their rightful place in the spiral of life.

Kathy Kouzmanoff

Living from the Center

16 Awake

From your core self, you look out on life more and more with the eyes of one who is truly awake. You no longer are so asleep, so on autopilot. You are living with a sharper awareness of yourself here and now. There is more concentration and more insight into life, both within and around you.

You marvel at the complexity of things as they are: your own living body, the majestic powers of your own mind, the ongoing struggles of the human heart, and occasionally, the infinite richness of Spirit.

You see the big picture and have perspective. You see yourself moving through the spiral of life, see others doing the same, and know we all are playing our parts. There is an inner delight in this waking up. You realize that you may be the center of things, but so is everyone else.

This high level of being awake to how things are gives you insight and, surprisingly, compassion. You have a basis for intuition and compassion for others. Your awakened self becomes the basis for love of everyone.

You can see more clearly what is yours and what is not. You freely see many possible responses to life's daily events. Nothing is alien. All is as it is. You see all, detached, but not uncaring. You are awake. You are aware. You are free.

17 Connected & Harmonious

Your return to your original Self is a return to the great unity in which we all share. Part of it comes from your compassionate connection to yourself, giving you a basis of compassion for all. Another part of your openness and harmony come from the very nature of your true Self.

Your true Self is the unifying ground of us all. Each person is but a manifestation of this shared Ground of Being. If we are all part of that great oneness, you cannot be alienated or isolated. There is only this overarching interconnectedness. You are part of all and all is part of you. There is no longer I and you, we and they, ours and theirs. Your true Self is the place beyond you and me, right and wrong, good and bad. There we meet in the one, abiding being that we are.

Connectedness and harmony are not a lack of boundaries or weakness. Your deep centeredness lives the paradox that combines strong personal presence with selfless, open connection. You let others have their place in the spiral of life. Your open heart is also an empty heart. It is empty of the little self that crowds out others. This emptiness is also its great fullness. Here rises the lavish magnificence of being itself. Living out of your true Self allows you to actually live in sync with others. You can experience this interconnection. It is real. It is harmonious connection everywhere.

18 Open

Living from your core Self is living with openness. Gone is the rigidity of insisting on how things ought to be. You are a like a visitor to the shore of a river. Life is flowing by, moment to moment. You remain, the alert and insightful one, on the riverbank, watchful of the river of life as it flows.

You can afford to be open. The inner strength of your core Self gives you your quiet center, your observing self. You are not being exhausted by the ongoing changes in currents of day-to-day living. There is no holding on. There is only flow, the endless rising and falling of being moment to moment. Observing what is, moment to moment, makes it apparent how you can hold onto nothing. This right relationship of your mindful receptivity to the river of life brings with it joy and freshness of spirit.

Your openness is with insight into how you came to this moment in time. Your openness is to tomorrow's reality as well, knowing that tomorrow depends on today.

You observe the vast richness of feelings, many of them contradictory. You see the pull of opposites all around you. You can let them be, with their tension effortlessly resolved within, by your core Self, by simply sitting in the quiet.

Your openness gives you a generous spirit, and a humble one. You are just part of the scene. Others need not be a carbon copy of you. They all have their story that brought them where they are today.

19 Paradox

Perhaps the most powerful dynamic of living from your core self is that you live out of two worlds, the world of time and space and the world of Spirit. This allows you to live with paradox. Paradox may be one of the surest signs that you are living from your center. Paradox is the worldview in which seemingly contradictory statements ring true. Paradox is an expression of time and timelessness coming together, providing the highest insight of logic. In fact, Henry David Thoreau went to far as to say that all truth is paradox.

Consider these seeming paradoxes of two famous writers. Gandhi said this about work: Everything that we do is unimportant, but it is important that we do it. Or what Jean-Paul Sartre said about freedom: Freedom is what you do with what's been done to you.

Gandhi's quote suggests that our limited viewpoint on reality misleads us. Sartre's suggests that we have freedom in our victim hood. Rumi is always trying to convey in his poetry that we are like fish looking for water, when we already are swimming in the ocean.

The drunk and the mystic are not far apart. Genius and madness are close. The mind and the heart both know truth. Passionate yearning and detached indifference are both of Spirit.

20 Observing and Letting Be

In your deepest self, you see that there is a place for all in the spiral of life. You acknowledge that there is a natural hierarchy of achievement and skills. You have no need to judge all levels as equal. You rather see that all levels have their developing and natural place in the spiral of life.

You see that all things exist and develop in their own due time. This includes yourself, each person, people, all cultures and every nation. You may throw your life energy into increasing knowledge and goodness. You may even perceive that the great arc of life moves toward greater good.

You observe. You don't judge. You can let be if you chose. You don't confuse having standards of increasing goodness with judgment or condemnation. There are developing places in the spiral of life. To observe is not to condemn.

You may at times experience an exhilarating harmony of body, mind, heart, soul and spirit. You may from time to time see yourself reflected in all levels of the spiral of life. In some way, you actually are the entire spiral of life. You are Everyman and Everywoman. And every man and every woman is you. In some way, you are everything. And everything is you.

Spiral of Life Dance

Yes, you are the dance of Spirit in time.

Infinity is dancing in you with time and space.

It dances as freedom and yearning,

Just so, and yes,

To be more, always more,

Reaching back from time,

To Itself beyond time,

And flowing back again,

Onto Itself, in endless delight.

And you know this dance.

You have been caught up

In its movement your whole life.

As have all in the spiral of life.

It is your very Self,

Dancing the dance of life.

And Infinity continues its dance everywhere,

Quickening all levels of being.

In these rhythms, Infinity knows and grows and

Everything is in love

With everything else.

Part 2 Levels of Development in The Spiral of Life

Kathy Kouzmanoff

Level 1   Responder

Responder Basics

Needy, Naïve, Narcissistic And Non-Aware

Body

(Non-Aware Ego/No Ego)

Basic Task: Physical and Emotional Survival

Basic Value: Neediness

Basic Belief: The World Is About Me.

Basic Problem: The World Is Not Just About Me.

Motto: *It's my way or the highway.* Or: *I'm nothing without you.*

41

21 Responder Description
Needy, Naïve, Narcissistic And Non-Aware

We all begin as "responders." We are born dependent, self-centered and unaware of how things work. In normal development, this stage lasts from birth to about fourteen. If you are an adult child, an adult who is stuck in the responder pattern, as a result of family dynamics or trauma, for example, you may not know you are at this stage. Maybe you don't even care. Responders' thoughts go something like this: "Forget it." "I don't want to deal with it." "It isn't true." "That's nuts." "It's your fault." "You don't understand." "You don't get it." "It sure isn't my fault!" etc., etc. Does any of this sound familiar? Notice how much denial and blame are in these statements, and how little there is of personal responsibility.

Usually a responder is one who gives a knee jerk, unthinking response to personal needs or to outside influences, hence the label "responder." At this level, you really don't think. You just react. You don't step back, and give yourself some space.

Others, who deal with life in a less needy and more effective, responsible way, don't have an easy time dealing with responders. And conversely, responders may not have a clue that they are hard on other people.

Admitting basic human needs, naming our feelings, considering the part we play in any given situation, these can all be scary for responders. So they may all be denied or buried, buried in withdrawal, work, drugs, food, drink, gambling, things, adventures, sex, etc. Self-centeredness and defensiveness rule in these cases.

Despite defenses of denial or addictive behavior, responders often experience strong fears, of being blamed, of being left out, of not being good enough. They may experience unnecessary deep shame, feeling guilty or inferior or scared or unworthy of the good things in life. This shame may cripple spontaneity and everyday enjoyment of life. Responders don't know how to fix themselves, so they look to others' approval to feel OK about themselves.

We have all seen grownups who act like children. The behavior almost looks crazy, it is so self-centered, needy, greedy, unaware or out of control. This is a responder in action. It is brutal to those around, and you can see the many kinds of violence done. It may be to just you, or to the environment, or to a family. Responder behavior can even engage large parts of a whole nation, as in times of civil unrest, political fighting or war.

Our highly individualized, consumer-oriented culture unfortunately encourages self-indulgence, excess and acting out. Personal indulgence looks normal to western culture, and is admired as the ultimate good life. But a lot of other cultures observe the excess and self-indulgence for what it really is. They can also see the damage that greed and excessive power do, especially to the poor and unaware.

Humor for the responder is often an effective way to avoid personal responsibility. Everything becomes a joke. Sarcasm at the expense of others is highly prized, the more caustic, the better.

Responders show a needy face when they are assessed in relation to common personality traits or preferences. Personality preferences between opposites, as listed below, (the preferences in a widely used personality indicator[13]), can all have a responder level of development, as suggested here.

- The responder *introvert* is imprisoned in loneliness. The *extravert* is socially awkward or excessively crude.

- The *sensing type* is self centered and needy in taking in details around them. The *intuitive type* is wildly uncontrolled and sometimes superstitious.

- The *thinking type* is unfocused. The *feeling type* is overpowered by feelings.

- The *ordering type (or judger)* goes from extremes of nonexistent order to rigid control. The *go with the flow type* (or *perceiver*) has flow that is chaotic.

Some basic personality traits, which are often viewed as indicators of a healthy personality, can show responder level development.

Emotional stability is lacking. There is anger, fear, regret, defensiveness, worry and anxiety.

Agreeableness is lacking. There is suspicion, contrariness and impersonal disregard for others.

Reliability is lacking. There is inconsistency, laziness and irresponsibility.

Openness to new experience has extremes. There may be outright hostility and closed-mindedness to any change experience may bring. Alternatively, there may be no limit on adventurousness and doing what you want. There may be no controls or respect for others, and an individual may swing in every which direction.

We all have been responders. We all know what it is like to be needy, naïve, narcissistic and non-aware. In times of stress, we may easily revert back to being a responder.

22 Responder Basic Task
Physical and Emotional Survival

The overriding need of a responder is survival! Physical survival comes first. Then comes emotional survival. Nature gives us very effective protections by which to survive emotionally. They are called defenses.

Of the various natural defenses available to us, the basic emotional one is denial. Denial is a defense against some threat to one's sense of self and it works by refusing to admit that there is a problem. Denial refuses to take any personal responsibility for a problem. Denial refuses to admit that emotional pain even exists.

Projection is another defense. We see the world as we are. So, if there is blame to be had, we see it in others, not ourselves. Projection says, There's nothing wrong with me, but there sure is with you! You're the problem. It's the pot calling the kettle black. It's seeing the sliver in our neighbor's eye and not the beam in our own. Projection makes you look good and others look bad. On the other hand, you can also project positive qualities onto the world, seeing good in others, because you are good and trustworthy.

Then there's the primitive thinking. You hope that childish wishes will get you what you need or want. You think the outside world owes you a living and is responsible for your happiness. You take little or no responsibility for making your own happiness.

In times of stress we can all revert back to these effective defenses of denial and projection and primitive thinking. They work so well to protect us that in times of need, we might regress and spontaneously use these defenses in order to survive emotionally.

23 Responder Basic Value
Neediness

Responders are like scared children. Childhood needs are inside somewhere, needs for love, attention, security, recognition or unconditional love. One's sense of self may be weak from instability in one's home, lack of praise or encouragement. There may be little or no accurately reflecting the child back to himself or herself, a process called "mirroring." Or maybe there is too much criticism, punishment, trauma, loss, anger and hate.

This lack of nurturing can lead to a sense of indefinable shame or a free-floating terror inside. They give you a pair of dark-colored glasses so to speak. The world as a result is a sad, lonely and frightening place. The pain gets buried, put outside the bounds of awareness. Yet the feeling of need keeps coming up, as does the sense of not fitting in, not being understood, not being good enough, not having enough or being safe. Past pain can bring up these feelings, even when things outside you are actually OK. That's how buried pain works. Responders often see the world through dark-colored glasses.

When you carry such burdens, you might go a little crazy, out of all proportion to what is going on in your life. Others see you are going a little nuts. Maybe you yourself see you are going a little crazy. Often, though, the responder doesn't think so at all. The issue at hand just seems intensely powerful, confusing and demanding, just as it did in childhood. Sometimes the responder is the only one wearing the dark-colored glasses.

Knowing that you have on the pair of dark glasses that are coloring your world can give you, as a responder, some freedom to take them off and try on a different pair.

24 Responder Basic Belief
The World Is About Me.

It can be the need for attention or the need to be right. It might be the need to act out, to do things your way. But it all boils down to one thing: It's all about you. Being self-involved and not valuing the other's point of view is sometimes called "narcissism."

Responders usually don't realize their total self-involvement. Their defenses do a good job of protecting them. Yet, others around them feel the effects of their self-absorption. Self-absorbed people feel so tiring to be around. They are an energy drain. They are closed-minded and inattentive to others. It may leave those around feeling empty inside or, at best, confused or frustrated.

"The world is all about me" has many disguises. It has a hard edge of power and control, but can be hidden in a velvet glove: "My intentions are to do good." "God is on my side." "My country, right or wrong." There are numerous other ways of holding yourself as superior, without respecting others' rights.

Anything can seem to take priority over the needs and interests of others. It can be my needs, my feelings, my ethnic group, my government, my music, my diet, my project, etc. My way is more high-minded, more politically correct, more fun, more cool or more desirable. My way is the only way!

Responders have only clear-cut, black and white definitions of right and wrong. There are no ambiguities associated with right and wrong, especially in the areas of personal needs, religion and politics. Anyone who disagrees with you may become the target of your anger, and its evil twin, self-righteousness.

Even caretaking can be self-centered. Fear of criticism may motivate power struggles or your good works may inflate your ego. You as caretaker may think you are the only one who can do the job well.

Of course, all this self-centeredness leads to much personal misery. The world is about me attitude works well for you, only in the short-term. Ultimately, it leads to confusion and discord and isolation.

A new attitude is, however, necessary, if one is to enjoy greater success in life. Others matter as much as you do. This change of attitude is the move toward cooperativeness and all of the rich pleasures that flow from it.

25 Responder Basic Problem
The World Is Not Just About Me

Learning that the world is not just about you happens painfully. You may find others annoying, selfish, ignorant and old-fashioned. They seem demanding, different and controlling. They just don't seem to "get it."

Alas, our good works, our charm and the schemes we plan don't always work. This may create a kind of serious disillusionment, as we realize the world is not "all about me." It is a kind of Paradise Lost. We have been forced to acknowledge that other people are separate from us, and that they have a point of view as well. Eventually, this crisis can become your opportunity for a better life.

Schooling and the hard knocks of daily living teach most of us that the world isn't just about us. We learn this naturally and gradually. This gradual development from a self-involved responder to a cooperative conformist takes time and experience. We come to realize that the world doesn't work too well if we remain totally self-involved. It hurts to let go of our self-centered illusions. It is a huge leap from self-centeredness to cooperation and mutual respect! New skills must be learned. In these new skills is a whole new way of seeing and doing life that is actually quite satisfying, and is the basis of further successes and joys!

26 Responder Motto
It's My Way Or The Highway. OR I'm Nothing Without You.

It's My Way or the Highway.

Controlling behavior is everywhere: controlling dads, angry bosses, bitchy women, snotty kids, faithless lovers, criminal gangs, oppressive governments, damning church leaders. Abuse varies from the gross to the subtle.

Having things your way is emotional survival for the responder and misery for everyone else. Children of rage-a-holics tell stories of cowering, hiding, trying desperately to please, so there wouldn't be violence!

These same children grow up with buried, destructive feelings of rage, sadness, confusion, depression, helplessness, fear, rejection, hatred and shame.

These can be the legacies of those who practice, "It's my way or the highway."

I'm Nothing Without You

Responders need others in order to feel good about themselves. They show little individual strength. If someone else needs them or loves them, then they feel that they are OK.

Personal boundaries are weak. Responders are happy if someone else is happy. Responders are sad if someone else is sad.

You as a responder are OK if other persons are meeting your needs. Other people are a kind of crutch for you. You give away responsibility for how you feel. Amazing, is it not, how these needy sentiments are the basis of so many popular love songs!

Responder Personal Development

27 Responder Motivation
Needy, Naïve, Narcissistic and Non-Aware

Motivation is the drive that gets you up in the morning, puts zest in your step and makes you live life with gusto. Motivation is interest, enthusiasm and reasons for doing things, the inner force or drive to act.

The most basic and instinctive motivation is for your own personal safety. Instinct motivates the "fight or flight" response in times of felt danger. Instinct and related emotions seem to do a good job, of protecting us physically and emotionally from anything that seems threatening. This self- protective impulse is in all of us, and it operates spontaneously.

Unfortunately, responders' motivations may be excessive and fear-based. Their instinct for self-protection is constantly on alert against various threats. And it often over-reacts. There is fear for one's physical or emotional safety. There may be fear of rejection, abuse or punishment. One fears being wrong, being different or not having enough money, food or control.

Shame, self-doubt or feeling powerless can also motivate a responder. They might hide away rather than assert themselves, and so are not able to meet their social needs. They are so afraid of being hurt, that they separate from almost everyone, even from the very people who can help, who care for them or love them. This isolating may lead to whining underachieving, blaming and depression. On the other extreme, responders may lash out in their powerlessness, being wildly over-reactive, achieving little and hurting those who love them.

Besides this tendency to be overly protective of oneself, there is the problem of self-centeredness. It often manifests itself in a person wanting everything done their way, to the exclusion of what others around them want. Responders can be control freaks. Opinions become orders or pontifications. Responders don't know how to have a genuine give and take with others. Responders may also need to be the center of attention in social groups. They demand attention, brag and monopolize conversations.

The unknown or the unfamiliar is frightening to responders. In religious terms, this means that there is only one divinely revealed truth, and there can be no other. Fundamentalists of any faith see other faiths as threats. Theirs is seen as the only true one, and it provides immense security, even after death! There is a need to defend oneself against those of other faiths and even to condemn them as heretics, heathens or infidels. This, in turn, can lead to violent hatred, self-righteousness, war and death.

Humor is often non-existent among responders, or it is at the expense of anyone who is perceived as a threat. It can reveal hostility and even latent hatred, being dark and willfully mean-spirited. The joke is often at the expense of others, a fact that only adds to the responder's pleasure.

Responders can also demonstrate a desire to please, be right or be rewarded, and they might achieve quite a lot. They are often dependent on these things to feel good about themselves. But, they often inject into the mix so much confusion and self-centeredness that their efforts at co-operation and belonging backfire. Conflict and alienation are frequently the result. In fact, their will to feel good about themselves may be further frustrated by their lack of social skills.

All this protective and unconscious motivation can be deeply irrational, creating urges that simply can't be met outside oneself. So one can never get enough of what one is after, with a desire for always more, more and more. It can be anything: more attention, control, power, stuff, food, drugs, sex, experiences, stimulation, excitement, fool hardy thrill-seeking, you name it.

We are meant to be free spirits. Motivation coming from dependency and fear leads to confusion, pain, anger, depression and helplessness. The responder is grasping for a more successful life. Self-destructive behavior to get free is common. How different it is for the conformist, who is motivated by achievement and belonging, and has the social skills to pull this off. Motivation is less protective. Individualists place even greater demands on themselves, demanding greater self-actualization, intimacy and authenticity in how they live. The conscient lives from a more inclusive place, where long years of refinement have led to an insightful mind and a universal heart.

28 Responder Identity
Self-Protective

Identity. What is it? Is it your individual history developed over a lifetime? Is it how others see you? Is it how you see yourself? Is it the part of you that changes? Is it the part of you that seems to be the same in childhood as it is in later years? Is it some combination of these?

Whichever of these you choose, identity seems to be the life-ring that we hold onto to keep ourselves afloat in the sea of life, providing a point of reference about ourselves in relating to others. Inner "self-talk" holds onto the favorable items that strengthen identity. It also represses the undesirable sides of us into the unconscious, creating our personal "shadow side." Sometimes the shadow can be a "bright shadow," created by repressing the positive parts of ourselves.

Identity for responders is a fragile thing. Excessive shame or self-loathing often marks their attitudes toward themselves. Their inner circumstances can be quite painful, depending on how effective their defenses are. The pain can be simply a loss of inner peace or contentment. It could be feelings of painful emptiness, or unexplainable restlessness or anger. Paranoia may develop as well, with the responder continually on guard against imagined threats, and his or her wariness can become greatly exaggerated. It is life behind the dark-colored glasses. Responders may feel unworthy of being loved.

Their natural defenses help responders to make it in a seemingly scary and heartless world. So this self-protection is ever at the ready, with bravado or excuses. Responders can overdo the defense thing and when people are turned off, responders feel powerless. Defensiveness and powerlessness are two sides of the same coin. They cause great confusion to those on the receiving end of these seemingly opposite behaviors.

Needing to be perfect can be another self-protective defense. Moral perfection or physical perfection, or a perfectly ordered home, or life, are all examples. In the responder's mind, being perfect puts him or her beyond blame, and hence free of anxiety, shame or guilt. It doesn't matter that personal perfection is actually nowhere to be found. When the search for it is on, the result can only be more anxiety, guilt, blame and failure.

The well-known Christian precept, "Be perfect as your Heavenly Father is perfect." is often misunderstood and misapplied by responders. To be perfect means that we should treat everyone equally in love, just as the rain falls equally on the just and unjust. Detachment and even-handedness in loving is this selfless ideal. We sometimes see it in good parents and teachers, or an inspiring leader or a selfless caregiver. Responders are often too needy and self-involved to provide such evenness in love.

The day almost always comes when you stop pretending that everything is all right. You want to find a way to improve. Count this day as the day when you awaken to a new identity! Finally, ineffective behavior and personal frustration will get the attention they need. Feel the urge to change! Welcome it! Seek help. This is the beginning of a new you!

Trust, if you can, the human support all around you. Let it flow to you. Little by little, you start seeing yourself as someone who is willing to be friendly and cooperate with those who have your best interests at heart. Little by little, you do your best every day, always looking on the positive side, seeing your future self, one successful in work and love. You begin to feel success and confidence build, perhaps all the way to becoming a positive force in other's lives. You also begin to experience a deeper place within yourself, one that feels good. It is a place that always is there, like a friend inside, helping you along the way, making your identity strong.

29 Responder Focus
Scattered

Focus is the ability to direct your attention. It is the key to your personal development. With it, you can concentrate your mind to think logically, take in details, manage your life, achieve goals and overcome obstacles. Focus also enables you to use your feelings to help you assess life situations. You sense when it is safe to open your heart in love and friendship and when it isn't. These mind/heart skills give you a sense of self-confidence and inner freedom.

Responders aren't very good at focusing. Their attention easily flits from one thing to another, all on its own. A scattered mind feels like too much stimulation, too many possibilities, too much pressure, too many contradictory directions, too many demands, impulses, obsessions and compulsions. In short, too much!

This scattered mind can be exhausting. You may be driven to keep up with the wild, restless movement that is in the driver's seat of your life. You may not be aware that your mind is leading you around, like a kite in the wind. You may try to keep up, probably not realizing how much is being asked of you, and how impossible it is to keep up. Your restless mind scatters you and wears you out.

Being driven and restless can also seem adventurous and a lot of fun. You do what you want to do, when you want to do it. You can get high satisfying the whims of the moment, without regard practicality, affordability or those around you. Crises are bound to develop from poor management of your life. Advertising and propaganda are aimed at just such minds, manipulating the chaos in them.

This restless adventure may seem like freedom, but is it? The mind, having this undisciplined life of its own is really in charge, not a free person. If you aren't aware of how wild the mind is, simply sit for a few moments from time to time and pay attention to its goings on, as it flits from this to that.

That the mind is easily influenced and impressionable is its admirable strength. That we are unaware of the mind's seemingly fickle ways is our unfortunate weakness. Much of human development is about becoming aware of yourself and learning to tame the scattered mind. It is the basis of time management and successful goal setting. As you become more self-reliant, you focus on things in a receptive, creative and integrative way. In maturity, regular inner practices help you achieve a clear and open being. Inner freedom, connectedness and joy are the result.

30 Responder Relationships
Needy

Relationships are a shared space where two individuals meet and create a third reality, their relationship. This shared space can be one of intense feeling, behavior and communication. A little bit of each person is given over to make this reality come into being. No one else knows what goes on in this shared private space but those involved, even though we love to guess! It could be anything from bondage to bliss. No two relationships are the same. New relationships are both frightening and thrilling, be they friendships, loves or shared projects. There is vulnerability and creativity for all involved. Relationships are a powerful and unique way for us to explore ourselves.

Needy relationships have partners who look for fulfillment in the relationship, rather than bringing fulfillment to the relationship. Because responders look to other people to feel good about themselves, they can become dependent on such relationships. They then try to control the relationship for their own needs. This dependency is not unusual, but it is nevertheless unhealthy and immature. It is not for mature people to rely on others for their well-being. We are born to be self-reliant, free spirits, and to be interdependent, rather than needy and dependent.

Dependency on a relationship for well-being can lead to excessive fear of losing an important relationship. Control becomes a substitute for healthy give and take. The need may be so great that one tries to make the other person over to meet his or her needs. This does not honor the individuality and freedom of the other person. If the person you are involved with doesn't fit your image of them, or resists your manipulations, you get upset. Your resulting agitation, anger and loathing at their independence might begin a cycle of controlling actions aimed at the other's submission.

Responder caretakers may be particularly vulnerable to this kind of enmeshment. They may give to be "appreciated" for what they do. Additionally, they run the risk of pleasing others at the price of ignoring their own needs. If they aren't appreciated, they get upset and often show their resentment. They are angry if others are late to their meals, or don't acknowledge extra efforts. Resentment is the clue that a caretaker may be doing too much or expecting too much.

Responder co-dependents look outside themselves for why they are the way they are. Blame for what goes wrong in life is put on those you are with, or your parents or schools or society. Being an agent for your own success, responsible for your life, is often foreign to the responder.

As a responder, you have little sense of yourself as an individual. You are often overcome with fears of abandonment, separation and isolation. Clinging to another in order to feel good about yourself may seem to a healthier person like an act of weakness and be annoying.

Responder co-dependency can show itself differently in unconscious patterns that Carl Jung found common to men and women. He called them the anima/animus in men and women. Being withdrawn, cold and brooding, with sentimental needs is often seen in men. Using bitchy anger, a know-it-all attitude where one size fits all, and emotional outbursts is often seen in women.

These patterns in one tend to set off the patterns in the other as well.

Overcoming needy relationships begins with a clear intention to be responsible for your own happiness. You look to yourself to be OK and relate to others in a mutually supportive way. If you need support, you seek it from healthy, independent people. They are all around you. You'll know them because they are gracious, generous and genuine. They can help you to overcome your grandiosity, secrecy, destructiveness, resentment and denial.

Gradually you learn to set boundaries between yourself and other people, to say no when things aren't right for you. You become an individual, free and strong. You come to relate to others in open give and take, not neediness and control. This is the beginning of cooperation, belonging, genuineness, and ultimately, unconditional love.

31 Responder Emotions
Anger, Fear, Greed & Need

Emotions are our friends. Really! Emotions are an instinctive, natural response of feelings to situations, giving you instant feedback and guidance to act. They act to protect us before we can think. They kick in a behavior to a situation that has proven to be useful for survival for millions of years. There are many emotions for many types of situations. In the wild, these emotions helped us survive. In modern, civilized life, we usually do not live in basic survival mode, so we need to fine-tune this otherwise brilliant guidance system. Learning refined emotional responses is emotional intelligence. Emotional intelligence is the basis of personal and social success.

Responders' emotions are more on the wild side. They haven't been tamed, and are often experienced in a strong, overpowering way. Some of these more common, powerful emotions are anger, fear, greed, need and desire for control. Any one of these can climb into the driver's seat and take control of us.

Trauma makes one's needy emotions even more intense, putting one on hyper alert. One is always instinctively scanning for attack, danger or the unknown. One is ready for anything! Always!

We do have natural defenses against our powerful, and hence, uncomfortable feelings. These defenses kick in naturally. These defenses may protect us personally, but adapt us poorly for social success. These defenses tend to repress, or make unconscious, our feelings. They include denial, projection, wishful thinking, self-centeredness, acting superior, perfectionism, black and white judgment, addictions, conversion of feelings to body symptoms, secrecy, manipulation, aggression and depression. When the defenses are overwhelmed, emotions may come out in explosive and inappropriate ways.

Taming our emotional wild side goes beyond these natural defenses. We can actually learn to work with our emotions and get smart with them. Consider these three stages on the way to refining your emotions.

First, protect yourself. Always choose safety. Leave a tense scene, where emotions are overwhelming you. Take a time out, calm down and think things through. Then try to put a name on the feeling(s) that you are experiencing. Naming what you are feeling is extremely important. It sooths and calms and validates your experience. Do self-talk to sooth yourself. If there are inner fears or helplessness or shame, name them and do self-talk with them as well, to calm them down.

Secondly, express yourself clearly. After you have cooled down and are back in control, you can say what you are feeling. Talking with another person or writing things out can be a big help. Putting emotions into words and expressing them weakens the power of the emotional part of our brains. You are now better able to pinpoint the problem and determine what you need to solve it.

Thirdly, enjoy taking action in a positive direction. Now you can more clearly give yourself what you need and ask others for what you need. Knowing the skills to get safety, express yourself and take action gives you a pattern to get free from overpowering feelings.

By doing these things, protecting yourself, expressing yourself and taking action, you will strengthen the power of your emotional intelligence. With such discipline in place, you can move away from emotional neediness to successful co-operation, self-actualizing genuineness and joyous, interconnected living. Along the way you are riding your untamed wild side, with greater and greater skill.

32 Responder Ethics
Getting Away With Things

Written in the human heart is a code of right behavior. We call it ethics. This "natural law" is something almost on the order of instinct. It is the basis of law and civilization itself. It has worked well, helping individuals and communities thrive. Right behavior counsels self-control and self-awareness, leading us to better understanding of ourselves and others. This, in turn, makes human cooperation possible. Ethics also reflects deeper, more subtle truths. Without moral refinement, the highest stages of growth are not achievable. Poor choices destroy trust, integrity and inner goodness, which are needed in order to end personal suffering and social injustice.

Responders may not care much about right behavior, or, sometimes, they care too much. Both of these extremes reflect their own often extreme state. Because responders are often desperate to survive, physically and emotionally, they simply act out. They don't think much about right or wrong. Responders are eager to get what they need or want, and may use whatever means it takes.

Getting away with things is something responders value highly. So is the cleverness that goes with it. On the other hand, responders may have an overly intense concern about being good. It often reflects a high level of emotional anxiety they have about their basic worthiness as a human being.

The small voice within that tells us what is right and wrong goes by many names. Call it conscience, The Golden Rule, the natural law, hard wiring or evolution. It seems like a contradiction that there is a natural law in the human heart, yet some people don't seem to live by it. Or they seem to stay stuck in patterns of responder ethics. Why might this be?

Religionists, sociologists, psychologists and other experts all offer their explanations for this. Some say that there is evil in the heart of a fallen, human race. Others say it is a permissive society, one's genes or poor child rearing. Overly harsh discipline or unduly high, or uneven standards may lead to confusion, resentment and even criminal violence. Trauma can keep one stuck in a needy place and keep one from maturing naturally. Gentle, reliable ways of guidance are obviously preferable, since they tend to enhance people's capacity for kindness, cooperation and empathy.

There are growth traditions that have bodies of teachings about the nature of human beings and how to live ethically or live well. Five major growth traditions are: Judeo/Christian/Muslim, Eastern, Indigenous, psychosocial and holistic science. Each of these growth traditions has a cohesive body of insight about how we ought to think and act. Each spells out a "right path." And each tradition has variations of orthodox and liberal views. There are, therefore, many resources for persons looking to live well.

The Jewish, Christian and Muslim traditions all have codes of behavior. The Ten Commandments are one such well-known set of rules. Christianity says the whole of the law is love. In Buddhism ethics is the Noble Path, with its four noble truths and eightfold path of right behavior, thinking and wisdom. In Hinduism there are yoga sutras of restraint in social relationships and observances to cultivate inner character. In the indigenous or native and pagan traditions, right behavior rises out of the traditional upbringing and rituals to connect you to nature and orient and grace your path. The psychosocial tradition emphasizes the stages of natural development at various ages. Questions of right and wrong morality rarely enter into psychosocial discussion. Yet the overlap of natural growth and morality is striking. The holistic science tradition integrates aspects of body, mind, heart and spirit into a cohesive whole. It doesn't teach right and wrong morality, but shows what scientific research says works well. It sees comfort and balance as the basis for good health and ongoing development.

It should also be pointed out that even growth traditions can be led astray. They can be corrupted through the misuse of personal power on the part of their authorities and through misguided political agendas. When personal power and political agendas are a driving force, and not right behavior respecting human dignity and rights of all, children are not cherished, women are dominated, minds are controlled, and violence is excused in the name of religion.

Discipline and right behavior go together over a lifetime. This is what needs to be taught to either the child or the responder. And it takes a caring, loving community to do so. Routines are the discipline of the successful student and young adult. Self-discipline continues as the basis of one's career, committed relationships and home life. In midlife, reflecting deeply requires disciplined use of time and thinking. Finally, spiritual maturity requires regular practices, keeping your spirit fresh, your love free and your bliss unbounded.

33 Responder Awareness
Physical & Self-Centered

Your awareness is what you are conscious of, through your mind, body or experience in the world. The great river of awareness is ever changing, and you are both ongoing participant and receptive observer. In this consciousness river of yours, flow sense impressions, body sensations, gut reactions, and your mental words and images about these experiences. This river of life that flows through you is awesomely managed by an inner control center, your mindful brain. It maintains your personal stability and flexibility within the larger context of continual change.

A responder's awareness is sometimes lacking in stability or flexibility. Instead, responder experience is not one of mindfulness, but of being overwhelmed. Needs for life's basics may be extreme or exaggerated. External goodies may be grabbed onto as a crutch to sooth anxiety. There may be imbalance about health issues as well. There may be excessive worry. Or responders may fail to take care of their health. They may have poor habits, and rely too heavily on the medical system to fix their problems.

Responders can find higher levels of awareness baffling and seemingly pretentious. They seem like meaningless riddles. To others, on the other hand, the needy, self-centered, awareness of the responder seems unstable. They seem too naïve, changeable, unpredictable or unreliable. If people point this out, the responder reacts with confusion, resentment and even anger.

Even though the responder's inner control center isn't always stable and flexible, his or her need for stability and flexibility is still real. Since they often feel overwhelmed within, they may look without for stability. Hate politics may appeal to them. It provides a place to put one's unrest. A strong personality with responder awareness, a will to power, high intelligence and persuasive charm can, in fact, be a very convincing leader in hate politics. History is full of them. And so are the media.

Another way to find stability for responders is through constant self-centeredness. You can almost see a responder's attempt to get a grip, as they talk only about themselves. A more stable person would be aware of others, show interest in them and have a more equal give and take.

Self-centered awareness usually means that you aren't taking other people seriously enough. It creates a tremendous alienation, as you risk turning people off, yet you aren't aware you're doing so. Or maybe you don't care. These limited skills in relating cause resentment, friction, arguments and, sadly, your own isolation.

Isolation and loneliness are profoundly painful, and may even be the proverbial bottom of the barrel. The good news is that the only way is up. Improving does begin by admitting into your awareness that, yes, there is a problem. I could do better. Just the awareness of your problem is already a move toward personal stability. Thinking about things more clearly gains you increased inner freedom. The clarity and increased inner freedom improves your part in relating to others. Success in the bigger world, where cooperation is essential, is on the move. Success breeds success. Your mindful awareness continues to grow in insight and subtlety, moving you along in the spiral of life.

34 Responder Wisdom
Painful Personal Boundaries and Suffering

There are hard realities in life to which there are no easy answers. The most baffling is the meaning of suffering. Yet we seek answers. Why? Why me? Why now? What did I do to deserve this? Why do the good suffer and bad don't? What can I do to stop the pain? Wisdom attempts to answer these questions of life's seemingly insoluble problems, giving meaning to the pain of personal isolation, limits, loss, illness, old age and death.

Some wisdom is better than others. One common-sense approach to suffering is to ignore it. Looking away from suffering may actually be quite useful. It is often expressed in the phrase, "Let sleeping dogs lie." Who is to say that such an approach isn't at times the most appropriate, or even wise? For most of us, this approach is often the most practical. We put suffering out of our mind by taking medication, staying busy, or taking a vacation. We distract ourselves with entertainment or with our work. These allow us to keep going, when otherwise our hearts might break.

Beyond ignoring suffering, you might deny that pain is a problem for you. Inflated thinking may take over, with attitudes such as, "Suffering is for sissies." or "I don't have problems, only solutions," and so on.

Responders' wisdom looks away in denial from suffering, even as it is aware of personal pain. This seeming paradox of denial and awareness that co-exist with each other is, of course, the beginning of true wisdom. For, without awareness of personal pain and suffering, how can one seek answers to overcome suffering? And, in the wisdom of things, a responder's suffering, and its denial, both protect the person from unbearable pain, and begin the transformative healing at the same time. Such is the paradoxical wisdom of Spirit life on the Responder level.

Responders look outside themselves for wisdom's answers. Wisdom within isn't usually where responders look for help. Responders usually don't know about the timeless, healing reality that is part of their own being. This reality, in which we all participate, is a teaching of the "perennial philosophy," which reflects common growth tradition teachings, from ancient times through the present. It is within where the Buddha went, as did Jesus, as do shamans, to find answers to overcome suffering.

Perennial philosophy is a timeless philosophy, common to most growth traditions. It teaches that there is a universal ground of being in which we all participate, and it is a part of being human, being one's core center or Self. It is transformative, wise, interconnected and doesn't end at the body's death. It is understood variously as Buddha Nature, God, the Great Spirit, Reality, the Self, the Tao, universal consciousness, etc.

Responders, however, don't trust their inner wisdom, and so they seek answers outside themselves. The answers to suffering that seem meaningful often reflect a responder's excessive shame and neediness, as reflected in their choice of religion or personal philosophy. They see suffering as a sign of the Father God's displeasure with wayward creatures. Their prayer is from a scared and needy child to this powerful, capricious God beyond. They feel shame, fear of judgment, of punishment and of hopeless, everlasting condemnation.

It is exceedingly frightening to admit that we are no longer in a blissful world of childhood or in our own personal paradise. It is a paradox that admitting helplessness is the beginning of personal power, wisdom and well-being.

But suffering alone will not make any of us wise. Suffering may break open our smug and self-centered hearts. It can just as easily close them even tighter in hard-hearted self-protection. Hitting a limit, admitting it and going beyond it, is the basic pattern of all personal growth.

Kathy Kouzmanoff

Responder Social Development

35 Responder Family
Family Of Origin, Committed Relationships And Support Circles

Family, loosely defined, is the people we identify with, who provide us a feeling of belonging, of kinship and who give us mutual support. With them, we create the synergy of kinship. For some, family is traditional, that is, it is strictly our family of origin or ethnic group. For others it's less conventional family, such as same sex partnerships. There are also communities of interest or need, "families" of a sort, such as religious groups, food coops or political parties. So, we can build family anywhere, on the golf course, in a chat room, or even around a radio program and its website.

Responder families are generally troubled. Chaos, blame and victimizing abound. Rules and roles are non-existent or are hopelessly confused. In some families abuse and dysfunction are obvious. In others, controlling and unsafe patterns can be more hidden and devious. The destructive impact on the family's members, nevertheless, still takes place. How do you know it is happening? You feel confused or empty inside.

Adult members, who are otherwise strong, may slip back into helpless, little kid patterns under dysfunctional family stress. There may be lack of cooperation, pouting, meddling, blaming, denial, control, judgment, negative talk, emotional outbursts or worse. Take good care of yourself. Family works better with members who care for themselves first.

Adults may mean well, but can be poor at mutual support. They may be too self-centered, needy and dysfunctional. They lose their focus of unconditional love for their children and get caught up in personal anger and hurt and show it to their children. They can be sullen, insulting and withdrawn, or excessively judgmental, blaming or punishing. Real caring is replaced by demands or formality.

Overly involved caretakers can become enmeshed with the other person's issues, be they illness, depression, drinking or poor management of resources or time. Rather than providing support, you somehow feel others' problems are yours to fix, to take care of or to control. This classic pattern of co-dependency just makes for more chaos and helplessness. You can easily get burnt out, angry, resentful and confused.

Authoritarian families demand loyalty. Problems may be denied or blamed on one member or on the outside world. We would be such a happy family, if it weren't for that kid. Our financial mess is because your spending is out of control! Such statements reflect helplessness and victimization. Defenses, denial, bravado, control, blaming and victimization take the place of open communication and empowered, problem solving.

A controlling person can dominate a family, be it parent, a child or an outsider. That person can dominate by constantly talking, claiming a higher moral or intellectual ground, or by showing irritation and anger with others. Being a person with a "problem," is a particularly menacing way to control a family. It's my way or the highway!

You may find that you are ignored, scapegoated or typecast in your family. You may be living someone else's dream or living someone else's problems. You may still be playing the same role you played in childhood. Because responders are so unaware, it may take a crisis of some kind to open their eyes to these patterns that bind them up into knots and keep them from becoming themselves.

How to cope with a dysfunctional family? Just get yourself free. How? Start with yourself. Take good care of yourself. Get the support of others. Learn to be honest with what's going on, to name your emotions and to set boundaries. Then you can support others in a sympathetic, fun and loving way, without losing yourself. Role models are around. Self-help books abound, as do therapists and support groups. If your intention is to nurture your family in a healthy way, you are already showing a more mature way of caring, and not mere neediness.

Your personal healing has enormous ramifications. How you live affects generations after you. The Bible speaks of the sins of the father being visited upon the sons.[14] The Native Americans speak of having an eye to seven generations in making decisions. Your strength of spirit affects those that are around you and those that come after you. Don't be blind to the fact that you matter a lot to others. Responders often don't realize that they matter to others. Life is not just about you, especially in family. As you become more content and happy and free, so will others.

36 Responder Politics
Personal Rights, Personal Power, Public Good, Public Safety & Public Office

Politics is a dance of power, between you, an individual citizen with rights and opportunities and the greater society, with power and authority over your rights and opportunities. Politics is about balancing personal rights and the public good. This dance, this continuous struggle between the personal and the public, becomes the art of the possible in politics.

On a micro scale, everything we do is political, from the way we dress, talk, the papers we read, the church we attend, to our personal behavior. They all have power and influence attached in some way, even if small. Even deciding not to decide is political.

On a macro level, your pocketbook and safety issues choose political candidates. In hard times, these issues are especially important and easy to manipulate. Your needs and fears can become the strongest of motivators. So voting campaigns can become targeted to get your vote, aiming directly at promising just what you need. With any integrity, such promises may actually be fulfilled. Without integrity, such promises are the basis of getting your vote, but little else.

Responder emotions can flavor campaigns. We are talking negative hostile and hateful. Attacks on opponents may be unfair and vicious. Truth is distorted, often with great cleverness, much to the glee of both speaker and listeners.

The politics of hate relies on fear of hard times and enemies at the gate. The masses get worked up to follow the bidding of those in power. Responders may be unaware they are being manipulated by very sophisticated propaganda and patriotic slogans.

Misuse of power relies on fear and manipulation as well. It is the politics of preemptive strikes and repression of civil rights.

This misuse of power happens in all areas of life, by family members, religious leaders or politicians. Charm and cunning can work their spells. High-sounding talk can hide the iron fist in the velvet glove. Your personal power is taken away, as you hear the talk of serving family, God and country. Responders don't see the double bind, as they react to the fine sentiments.

Hate, not reform, can also affect the criminal justice system. Criminals become society's scapegoats, not fellow human beings who owe a debt to society and need to have a new start. A hard heart leads to new definitions of what is criminal as well, with harsh sentences attached to basically victimless crimes.

Even an entire continent can suffer from responder politics. In Africa, there is immense poverty in many countries, as public monies go into private pockets, and not the education and economy and infrastructure. Greed, the lingering burden of a colonial heritage and ancient hatreds between tribes and factions, keep countries from coming into their own.

Hard heartedness can look on the mentally, physically or economically disabled as disgusting, and dismiss their needs as low priority. Civilized societies can be judged by how they care for their poor and needy. We are talking health care, job training, unemployment compensation, child welfare protection, disability support and care for the retired and aging.

Responder politics is based on need and fear. Politicians manipulate it, to their advantage. The human mind and heart know there is a better way, more selfless and cooperative. So we strive for greater equal rights, better universal education and economic opportunity. We know that these are the basis of personal power and peace, both at home and abroad. These high sounding ideals inspire the human spirit to work for a more just world. Through them, we overcome our frightened and fragile selves, and give what we can to make a better world.

37 Responder Religion/Arts
Art, Philosophy, Psychology and Religion

There are many paths that show how to live the good life, to be your best, to be fully alive. Speaking broadly, society offers us the paths of arts and aesthetics, philosophy, psychology and religion. Religion provides institutionalized teachings on the nature of reality and how to live well. But, whether it is the arts, logic, human development, God-based or non-theistic religions, you have choices at life's every turn.

At the heart of each of these is an attempt to better yourself, or live well in the larger world. In institutionally held traditions, we seek both teaching and community. These enhance the beauty, truth and goodness of our lives.

Aesthetic taste for responders is often sentimental, deeply sweet, cozy and comforting. Religions can sometimes pick up this style. They can be sweetly sentimental, providing comfort to those in search of solace. Art styles can also be glitzy and glamorous, bright and shiny, highly emotional and romantic.

Even the growth traditions of religion have a responder level. Responders can feel unsure of themselves, anxious, unworthy or isolated. They may experience weak personal boundaries. They can find a tradition that seems like a comfortable fit for them. Being right is really important. It can be to soothe one's guilt-ridden soul, satisfy a teacher, master a field of study or be right before God.

Traditions that have the "right answers," meet the needs of responders. These teachings tell you that God himself revealed their right answers. They guarantee a path that will lead to an eternity of happiness. Should you get off the path, these religions offer the right behavior and right rituals to get you back. They keep you on the good side of an easily angered, demanding, scorekeeping God, who sees all and can act heartlessly with humans. Such religious certainty is all deeply reassuring to a responder.

Such religion can also have a harsh edge to it, where authority is everything. There may be demands for blind acceptance of what is taught. There are eternal consequences of heaven or hell attached to this obedience. Someone who believes differently is a threat to the group. Those who are different are wrong, condemned, shunned or even killed. Not all religious authorities crudely confuse personal power and religious teachings. But those who do, are easily prone to violence, justified in the name of God.

Sometimes a responder feels so strongly about having found "the answers," that they can't help but try to convert others to their truth. Their self-limiting projections now believe theirs is the only right path for others. Preaching is done with religious fervor. It is often against the sins of the flesh and the evil of the unbelievers. Condemnation is practiced, and with passion.

Responders may have a deep need to be loyal to their religion, such as the one of their childhood. They may never question it. Or they may fear that if they leave, they too will be abandoned, by the group or even by God.

Responders often take spiritual writings literally. In religious teachings, stories and symbols are often meant as metaphors for personal change and spiritual realities. Fairy tales, mythology and sacred imagery are examples. Instead of seeing stories as teachings about the inner life of soul and Spirit, responders tend to interpret them as historically true, taking them at face value. This approach is amazingly common. It lumps both history and teaching stories into one category.

So, responders find what they need in growth traditions that perfectly match their place in the spiral of life. Where self-control and cooperation are stronger, traditions emphasizing more maturity beckon. People who are seeking personal meaning may seek traditions valuing independent religious thought. They may seek to consciously unify the individual self with the transcendent Self. Finally, those with direct experience of timeless Spirit, look to communities that honor this mystical union.

38 Responder Sex/Closeness
Eroticism, Sex, Connectedness, Love, Communication,
Masculine and Feminine Orientation

What is this thing called love? The instinct to find closeness, and intimacy, is powerful, relentless, surging, urging, reaching and connecting. And love is frightening, so powerful it can drive us to do the outrageous. Against its power, we try to gain some control, repressing, denying or otherwise building defenses against being too close. Yet the erotic, the felt sense of connection, continues with great force. Life keeps being charged our entire lives with this delectable energy of connecting. The object of our affections may change as we change. Yet the urge to connect never stops.

Connecting for responders is often a frustrating and baffling experience. But they don't know why. Their limited self-awareness, social skills and self-centeredness keep them from knowing how to connect. This often results in confusion, pain and loneliness.

The most common way to connect is through talk. One may be interesting, witty and even charming. But listeners may not be able to get a word in edgewise. They can feel strangely empty, bored, or angry at being on the end of such a one-sided conversation.

Another way we attempt to connect is through fashion. Clothing signals who is in and who is not, if you know the codes. Dress may tell others if you are available sexually, or if you are not. Fashion and sex are deeply intertwined, especially for the young. It often dictates dressing like wanton, sexual creatures. This creates confusion. One may want to look fashionable to others, but not want to fuel raw desire.

Many responders are deeply uncomfortable and awkward around sex, the urge, the arousal and the bodily expression of sexual energy. They may give mixed messages, wanting to seem sexy, and so, act sexually provocative, telling off color jokes in the wrong company, or going around half-dressed, to the discomfort of others. Fear of real intimacy may lead to casual sex.

If one enters into a sexual relationship, deeply powerful emotions are opened up. This bodily intimacy is instinctively tied to one's deepest, most powerful emotions. To protect against such vulnerability, partners may "objectify" sex, telling themselves that they are turning off their feelings, and concentrate on the merely physical.

Sexual domination is common and can take place from the crude to the subtle. Consider the following:

- A sex saturated, mass culture

- A youth driven culture, that overcharges the young and the beautiful with sex, while denying its power to the mature and the physically imperfect

- Unwanted sexual flirtation, dirty jokes or physical touching; unwanted by the other, it is all abuse.

- Don Juan lothario types, who are good at seduction, and charm their victims, all for the thrill of the chase and the glory of the conquest

- Older, "worldly-wise" predators, who sexually manipulate the young or naïve or powerless for their own satisfaction; They may simply dominate or rationalize, exploiting unequal positions of authority or power.

- One sex dominating another through control tactics of money, the law or social codes

When sexual connections become complicated, difficulties may start to emerge. Masturbation may become a substitute for relating, leading to feeling whole for the moment, but leading nowhere in relationships. Perversions may substitute for mature relating. Pornography becomes an exciting substitute for the thrill of loving another. These sexual patterns do not satisfy one's need for real connection. So they just fuel more desire. Sex may become an addiction and the sexaholic is born.

Eventually, these frustrating, alienating attempts at connecting lead to turnoffs and damage in others. They lead to isolation in oneself and trouble with the law. That all this sex is unsatisfying because true connection doesn't occur, is utterly baffling to the responder. The responder has come to the end of the road, needy, non-aware, and in a whole lot of pain.

Such great pain must break through in a sexually frustrated responder in order to finally understand that there is a problem with responder sex. The loneliness becomes too much to bear. The wasted money, time and energy finally take their toll, having led to broken and destructive relationships, walks on the dark side, perversions, addictive behavior or trouble with the law.

The world is not just about you and your desires. Until the responder has the realization that self-centered sex is not enough, there can be no moving on. Going it alone hurts. It hurts yourself and it hurts those around you. Good connecting and good sex begin by taking the other into account, and for the responder, it is the next great quest in love and sex.

*

39 Responder Social Situations
Food, Shelter, Clothing, Cyberspace, Society and Time

We are social fish, swimming in a vast sea of social life, which provides us both changeable cultural opportunities and ongoing social structures. In this social life, of culture and social structures, we live, move and have our being. In most modern societies, we can find most anything we want. Social life is all things to all people, providing a mirror for what we value and who we are.

Let's consider stuff, material things. In the mid 1800's, Ralph Waldo Emerson wrote, "Things are in the saddle, and ride mankind." One wonders what would he say today!

There is a self-indulgent attitude that says, If it feels good, do it. Decisions only affect you. In this way, we are encouraged to have immediate gratification, and to live way beyond our means. Sales and marketing are pitched for a "must act now" response, through sale prices and time limits. Get yours while you can. Supplies are limited. Opportunity only knocks once. The world is your oyster. You not only own the road. The world is yours for the taking.

Responders plan their time and involvements poorly. They may be bored with too little to do, or be desperately confronting crises and unmet desires. Often worn out from such poor planning, self-indulgence and over-extension, they may come to social situations stressed out, feeling hungry, angry, lonely or tired. The AA programs use these four words to form an acronym HALT, urging good self care, and a stop to socializing, until one's needs are met in these areas. Food and drink can work really well to sooth stress, loneliness and boredom. Responders use them as a means to do just that, but perhaps without awareness or to excess.

Media habits may also be excessive, demanding continuous stimulation or gadget replacement, often taking on an addictive quality. Music, cable television or an electronic gadget may be essential to the "good life."

Going to school and getting a "good education" may or may not be appreciated by a responder. They may be unaware how training opens doors and connections. They may lack the personal drive to develop their talents. They may be overcome with personal problems, and not be able to give schooling their full attention.

Health care systems are used, often in times of crisis, to fix the results of dangerous living, a polluted environment or over-indulgence.

So, the responder finds himself or herself in a sort of private kingdom of personal indulgence and excess. The world is all about them. It works for a while. But its complications, expense and isolation start to feel constricting. They want more from life. This feeling of oppression is just what is needed to inspire one to try to relate more successfully in society, so as to live with more true abundance.

40 Responder Work
Money, Livelihood, Hobbies, Special Interests, Daily Routines, Useful Activity

To be useful, to be creative, to better the way you and others live is at the heart of work. Dr. Sigmund Freud thought that work, along with love, is what life is about. Work is useful activity. For the responder, work may often be, at best, a necessary evil.

Work habits, originating from years of choices, for responders are often are muddled or self-defeating. They frequently lack focus, orderliness or discipline. The non-aware responders may wonder why others are "picking on them." They feel confused, discouraged and even depressed at their lack of success and accomplishment.

Fear can lead to behaving well in the workplace. You want to do the right thing, because you may lose your job if you got caught cheating or stealing. Likewise, you follow the rules carefully, so that you don't make your boss angry. It sounds a lot like the world of powerless children.

Low self-confidence leads to low expectations, leading to frustrations and failures in the work place. Nothing succeeds like success, and nothing discourages like failure. The befuddled responder, who lacks confidence, is often discouraged, seeming lazy and incompetent. This self-defeating, vicious circle traps one in a dead end. Indeed, it is when expectations are high, perhaps from others around the responder worker, that the fire of determination may kindle a new beginning.

Yet responders can also be slackers, sometimes not giving more than they have to. There is no real satisfaction in the work. The attitude is, Only a fool works hard. If you can, let someone else do the dirty work. Try to do as little as possible. Try not to work at all.

Responder workers look to the workplace to meet their personal needs and little more. They hesitate to identify with or bond with fellow workers, management or even customers. Responder salespersons may use a "Con 'em" attitude: A fool and his money are easily parted. Let me help you do it.

Work can be used in an addictive way, to cover up personal pain, or give one a feeling of self worth. Also, work can get out of control, with too much stimulation and excitement causing a manic high, followed by a depressive crash. This cycle is very common in cultures that stress ambition.

Lack of planning may lead to rushing, too much to do, doing the unimportant rather than the important. First things first for responders means acting on what they feel like doing, not on what really matters most. As a result, responders live with urgency and crisis. They may even think life is just one crisis after another.

On the other extreme, responders can over focus their work. Precision, order and predictability rule to an extreme. Their sense of control, when in an authority position, can be excessive, with little care given to what others think or need who work for them.

Responder managers can see their workers as "beneath them," as cabbage heads to be manipulated. They try to pay employees as little as possible, and provide as few benefits as possible. Workers are a commodity, not human beings, who are to be treated with fairness and dignity.

Depression and exhaustion may reflect being on the receiving end of poor working conditions, with low wages, long hours, and not enough money, time or energy to make ends meet. Work can feel like enslavement under such conditions. Human dignity is compromised. Holding back may be a means to survive, under overwhelming demands.

That all of these behaviors and attitudes lead to a dead end is pretty obvious. Unhappiness and envy of more cooperative, skilled and productive workers may be a signal from within you that it is time to change. Your spirit yearns to break free of its chains. It's time to move on to bigger and better things. Work may no longer just be a necessary evil. You may actually be inspired find a useful way to improve your work life, step by small step.

Level 2   Conformist

Conformist Basics

Smart, Savvy, Sassy and Successful

Mind & Heart

(Ego)

Basic Task: To Take The Role Of The Other
Basic Value: Doing And Belonging
Basic Belief: If I Am Good, Things Will Be OK.
Basic Problem: I am Good and Things are not OK
Motto *He Who Dies With The Most Toys Wins.   OR   You're nobody 'til somebody loves you.*

41 Conformist Description
Smart, Savvy, Sassy And Successful (Mind and Heart)

This conformist life of doing and belonging starts as a child. You are learning all along to be smart, savvy, sassy and successful. It is the basis of your successful, young adult life. The conformist stage, developmentally, is from about age 15 to 35, although it can break through earlier or last longer. So, what, exactly, does this conformist learning entail?

You learn to control your socially unacceptable responder side, managing expression of strictly personal needs and emotions. You learn quickly, through outside rewards and punishments, what is acceptable and what isn't acceptable in the larger world. You are developing your thinking and social skills.

You have begun to learn to "take the role of other." You are beginning to understand what society wants from you, that is, where other people are 'coming from.' And you can also communicate to others accurately that you understand where they are coming from. This is the foundation for building mutually satisfying relationships.

Most importantly, your self-control is providing you the ticket to success. You are learning to practice "deferred gratification," in order to meet a goal. This means you can put off enjoying yourself now, for a greater good in the future. You can study rather than party. You can save for a home rather than spend all your cash.

For the conformist, there is a lot of coming and going, doing and belonging, giving and receiving. You give of your time, your talents and your affection, and in turn, you receive money, status recognition and belonging. You are realizing that your desires and behaviors are merging nicely with socially acceptable behavior.

In developing the doing and belonging sides of your personality, you are creating the groundwork for a lifetime of "having it all." Head and heart, these are the two sides of personality that are in every person, the masculine achieving side, and the feminine belonging side.

This doing and belonging creates a kind of socially acceptable you, one that conforms to conventional beliefs, a need to look good, be successful, be correct, and "save face" in times of difficulty.

Your responder feelings of inferiority are giving way to taking initiative and being productive. Your responder pattern of isolating is giving way to intimacy. Religious conformity is helping you to overcome your indifference or hostility to others. As you learn to play social roles by proper rules, you are aware there is a certain conflict between these and your personal, less controlled side. To help overcome the tension between social roles and personal reality, your humor pokes fun at the establishment. There are jabs at the establishment, the mother-in law, the boss, the church, and of course, sex.

There can be a dark, shadow side to getting ahead. For example, you may become so driven, that your pattern becomes one of alienating determination, or deviousness, expedience, or sheer willpower. You may use belonging to your advantage, taking on false identities, becoming overly "phony" in order to belong. Your self-respect may depend too much on your outward success. You may experience depression or anxiety if you cannot conform to excessive outward standards. Also, because you are sometimes willing to compromise your integrity, a certain cynicism can set in. Conformists can think that cynicism is very smart, savvy, and generally, a cool attitude to have.

Individualists and conscients may see your conformist success and be pleased for you. Responders might see conformists as uppity, overpowering, or way beyond a responder's abilities. Sometimes individualists see limitations in the conformist stage, seeing it as a trap, an excess, as something to go beyond, to use sparingly, or to reform.

Conformists show a cooperative face when they are assessed in relation to common personality traits or preferences. Personality preferences between opposites, as listed below, (the preferences in a widely used personality indicator[15]), can all have a conformist level of development, as suggested here.

- The conformist *introvert* values positive thinking and love. The *extravert* masters the rules and roles required for success.

- The *sensing type* develops keen observation. The *intuitive type* uses hunches to be proven right or wrong.

- The *thinking type* develops logic. The *feeling type* shows socially acceptable emotions.

- The *ordering type* (or *judger*) sets up daily life by goals and good time management. The *go with the flow type* (or *perceiver*) instinctively balances personal needs and social demands.

Some basic personality traits that are often viewed as indicators of a healthy personality can show conformist level development.

Emotional stability is successful. Your emotions are in check overall. There is control of personal feelings. Being socially acceptable is valued.

Agreeableness is present and highly valued. It is built on self-control. On it is built cooperation, trust and right and wrong.

Reliability can be counted on. It shows in being hard working, consistent and responsible.

Openness to new experience is strong, but guarded. You stay within certain social circles, within acceptable limits, where you feel understood and supported.

42 Conformist Basic Task
To Take The Role Of The Other

Taking the role of other has two parts to it. One is personal self-control. The other is empathy for the other person and showing your empathy.

Personal self-control happens gradually as you grow up. People around you let you know over and over what is acceptable and what is not. The messages are relentless, and sooner or later, you begin to control impulses and feelings that are self-centered, and to show your more cooperative and socially desirable side.

Your own experiences of balancing strictly personal desires with the demands of society, give you a rich background to reflect upon. Your experiences can act as a basis for understanding others, assuming that we all are similar in some basic ways. This is an appropriate basis for empathy, for acknowledging and sympathizing with another's point of view. And your behaviors reflect your understanding. You can say you understand, you can feel with, and so work together. This is what we call "taking the role of the other," and it is how we become cooperative and are able to develop a sense of belonging.

Alas, our social conditioning may also lead to personal repression, with the unacceptable being denied or becoming unconscious in us. This sometimes leads to double standards of saying one thing and doing another. These double standards are confusing and the cause of much grief and cynicism in social relations. It is only in later years that we awaken to the parts of us that we repressed, often with much relief and humor.

43 Conformist Basic Value
Doing And Belonging

The powers of both the mind and the heart yearn to be fully recognized. These two energies of doing and belonging can also be spoken of as masculine and feminine energies. The masculine seeks to achieve, to do and to perform to standards outside oneself. The feminine seeks natural kinship, feeling deeply, becoming attached and knowing that it belongs.

You may or may not think of yourself as having a masculine and feminine side. To be male is to be born with a male body. To be female is to be born with a female body. But both share masculine and feminine traits. If you are to be fully successful, you need to develop your doing, masculine side and your feminine, belonging side. One is of the mind. The other is of the heart. The conformist aims for competence and accomplishment on the masculine side. On the feminine side, the conformist develops friendship, deep personal love and family life, and generally lives cooperatively.

44 Conformist Basic Belief
If I Am Good, Things Will Be OK

Along the way you learn what it takes to get along. Slowly you begin to adapt your behavior to the demands of society. But there is a certain hidden message in this conditioning. If you are good and conform to the standards you are taught, you are a good person, and everything is going to be OK. You are going to have a successful and happy life.

So, for you, there is a right way and wrong way to do just about everything. In your early years at home you will learn proper ways of how to eat, do personal grooming, and how to converse with others. You also learn how to bond with your caregivers, and then repeat that pattern with others, to form bonds of attachment with siblings and friends.

You go to school and learn to share, to play in groups. You learn about doing things the right way, how to write, to read, to speak and to dress. You learn subjects such as math, art, music and sports. These all reinforce conformity and group belonging. You learn to conform, to hold acceptable beliefs about right and wrong, and, perhaps, even about some of the deeper life questions such as the nature of good and evil, and even the nature of God.

You are learning the "right" things to do and believe, to be smart and successful. The world will reward you, because you are so good, and you're doing things the right way. Things are going to be OK. This is the message behind the conformity that is demanded of us in daily life.

45 Conformist Basic Problem
I'm Good and Things are not OK

You are good, play by the rules, do as you are taught, try to be a good person, and things still do go wrong. Things are not OK!

Murphy's Law cynically says, If things can go wrong, they will. Well, maybe not always. But things do go wrong regularly, and bad things happen to good people too!

Bad things are happening, even to you, a good person if how you might feel. It isn't supposed to be this way. This seems contrary to what you were taught. It's a basic violation of the social code that says, If you are good, things will be OK. What are you supposed to think when this happens? Sometimes it seems that there is nowhere to turn, no way to cope, no clear guidelines on how to act or what to believe.

Your confusion and pain force you to look beyond mere conformity, to seek a higher viewpoint from which to reconcile the conflict you are confronted with. But, it seems that these answers have to come from a place you may not have accessed before, one not connected to a world so unfair and arbitrary.

You need to determine what is truly good for you. You are being forced to discover your own path to something more real, more enduring.

46 Conformist Motto

He Who Dies With The Most Toys Wins. OR You're nobody 'til somebody loves you.

He who dies with the most toys wins.

The game of material acquisition is that played by the capitalist and capitalist culture. You win the game when you have lots of "toys." And, the toys need to be the latest version, the latest fashion and latest gizmo.

In a culture that values material goods, it isn't often disputed that having the most toys makes you a winner. A quick glance around you at your possessions makes it possible to assess how successful you are in this game.

You're nobody 'til somebody loves you.

Romantic love glorifies falling in love. It is that fateful attraction of one person for another, in which you feel a sudden, irresistible connection between you and another. You are smitten, hopelessly and happily. There is a mysterious feeling of being completed by the other person.

If you listen carefully to popular love songs, you may notice how often the message is a variation on the theme: "You're no body 'til somebody loves you. You're nobody 'til somebody cares."

You have found the person with whom you belong. As a conformist, your love is less from neediness, and more from the magic of finding the right person and feeling the magic of love.

Conformist Personal Development

47 Conformist Motivation
Doing and Belonging

Consider what makes you tick, what gets you out of bed in the morning. That energy and drive that is you, your motivation, alas, isn't entirely under your control. Part of your life force has its own inner agenda, coming from the unconscious. You have also been shape-shifted for most of your life, as well, by outside forces. Some have hurt you and made you want to stay in bed, or maybe get out and hurt somebody. Other motivations have given you the sweet thrill of success, feeling that you are somebody, that you belong, and it's practically effortless to start a new day.

Conformists may or may not be aware of these complex and conflicting motivations within them. Mostly, conformists are driven by an all-embracing desire for personal success. This is, however, an odd, contradictory situation. On the one hand, society encourages you to develop into your best self, to use your talents, interests and abilities. On the other hand, personal success is keyed to the need to get along, to conform. And, to get along, you go along, with the existing rules of the roles that you take on. So, at the very core of personal success, of being smart and successful, there is the built-in contradiction of self-interest and social conformity.

This dual motivation serves both you and society well. It is the basis for sound family, public education, common beliefs and good government. It also fuels the engine of the economy, by encouraging you to buy, buy and buy, so you can continue to look good in every respect. Successful conformist motivation thus benefits personal achievement and the larger society. You fit in. Your self-esteem is strong, because it is reinforced by your successes.

Conformity can sometimes be skin deep, however, leaving you devious, and full of clever schemes. You may create good appearances, but also rebel against all that conformist life stands for, creating inner confusion for you, and complications for those around you. In addition, responder motivation sometimes may want to skip conformity, jumping right into being an individual. Alas, persons with poor social skills suffer a tremendous handicap and are still responders.

So, you've got your career, your home and your family. Your doing and belonging are coming along. You join the groups that are right for you, that support home, school, church and community. You've played by the rules.

Still, for many, there comes a time when living by the rules is no longer enough. You outgrow it all. You get bored. You become disenchanted, with your spouse, your work. It suddenly feels like you are living life by external standards, by someone else's standards. Also, in spite of playing by the rules, you don't always come out ahead. Bad things happen. Your children get into trouble. The economy goes bust. There are sickness, war and natural disasters. You pay a high price. The religious beliefs you adhered to don't make much sense anymore, either.

You are at a loss, feeling betrayed. You become cynical and angry, and don't know where to turn next. This is understandable and only natural. But now comes the real challenge. How are you going to respond when the rules don't make sense any more? Your disillusionment and pain, which break the conformist agreement, may motivate you to seek a new direction. You have outgrown being smart, savvy, sassy and successful. Conformity served its purpose for a part of your life. Now it is time to go deeper, to become deeply reflective about your life, and get painfully real. Who are you, really? What do you as an individual really want and need to make your life whole again?

48 Conformist Identity
Conventional Roles and Rules

In conformist identity, who you are over a lifetime, how others know you or how you see yourself, is taking on a smart, savvy, sassy and successful personality. The village that it takes to raise the child does its best to develop you into a cooperative, useful and successful member of society. Unless you are stuck for some needy reason in the responder stage, you are naturally thriving with a strong and healthy sense of yourself. You really enjoy your successes.

You want to be well thought of, to be known as a person taking on roles in life that bring prestige and recognition as a "successful" person. Your self-esteem is tied into this identity, playing out your roles well, knowing the rules and living by them to be a success. To master this level of development, you need look no further than mastering the rules and roles that you have chosen for yourself or that society expects of you.

Society expects you to do your work well. It expects you to be a contributing and capable participant in daily life. Ralph Waldo Emerson commented insightfully on this, saying society really doesn't care what role you play, but only that you do it well.

It is normal and desirable for things to run smoothly. If they don't, if you have a lot of trouble getting along with people, or don't communicate effectively either you or those around you are not at the conformist stage.

In a way, conformist identity is more about society than about you. You may choose a career or relationships that seem right for you. Yet you are expected to follow the law, to honor your parents, to be true to your friends and loved ones. You are held accountable for your professional work as well. You meet your obligations as parent. You are an informed voter. You know and support the teachings and values of the growth tradition that you identity with, living by its rules. You are a good neighbor. You dress for success. You look good. You eat well. You drive the cars that most people like. You are a good team member. You create. You achieve. You are focused and committed. You work hard and play hard. Your life is full and rich.

A healthy sense of doing and belonging is a good thing. Don't let anyone tell you that it is a bad or egotistical thing. Success is the very basis of your contentment, of having happy relationships and living in a well functioning society. When you are in the higher levels of individualist and conscient development, you enhance your strong and healthy ego with added perspectives. The old saying applies: *You can't become nobody until you become somebody.*

Until one day, it happens. You simply get tired of it all, the conformity, the rat race, the endless demands, other people telling you how to dress, how to think, how to live your precious life. You seem to be losing yourself. You don't know who you are anymore. All this doing and belonging, playing by the rules and roles that society values, seems meaningless, like dry straw. All you want to do is to break free.

Some inner force is pushing you into shedding this conformist identity that now seems way too small. You are being pushed into a much bigger world, being urged to find out who you really are, and what really matters to you personally.

49 Conformist Focus
Intensifying Concentration

Focus is the ability to direct your attention in the way you choose. For the conformist, the ability to concentrate one's attention is absolutely key to being smart, savvy, sassy and successful. How is it key? It is the basis of getting what you want, in work or love. Focus allows you to think logically and attune to others emotionally. This deeply enhances your sense of internal freedom and well-being, creating a basis from which to experience wide-ranging interconnectedness and even joy.

Is all this possible? Yes.

The practices of intensifying focus go by many names in various growth traditions. In conventional society we talk about focus, time management or success training. In psychology we refer to strengthening ego. In religion we talk about building character. In the ox-herding stories of the eastern Taoist/Zen tradition, these practices are referred to as taming the ox.

The mind is a wandering gypsy, full of unbounded spirit, universal sympathies and aristocratic freedom. It is the great dream machine, the autonomous participant in a universal consciousness, and the creator of breakthrough theories and improbable accomplishments. Such astonishing powers are between our own two ears! The mind even provides its own inner system of stabilizing all of this flexible potential, through its capacity for mindfulness.

So, for the conformist to narrow down all this vast potential into intensifying one's personal focus is in itself a major achievement. It takes years of social conditioning to forge this socially favored path of intensified focus. The mighty brain doesn't forget its larger than life nature, however, as we learn to narrow our focus. The mind sneaks in its escapes into its wider horizons through luscious daydreaming and simply wandering where it will. These forays of the wandering monkey brain may make more sense than we know. This balancing act goes on from minute to minute, in a mind that integrates its many capacities. It is fluid, adaptable, creative, stable and capable of doing your conscious bidding.

So keeping focused on one's chosen objectives is really very challenging. You are giving up part of the present to live in the future. It requires a sharp focus of your minds' eye to see this future. And to achieve your goals, you have to bring them into focus over and over again. This is intensifying focus.

You can do all of this only if you have a key factor of emotional intelligence, which is the capacity to delay present gratification for future payoff. Give up the marshmallow now for the bigger payoff later! If you can keep the sharply defined goal, break it into smaller achievable parts and follow disciplined routines necessary to accomplish the tasks and achieve your goal, the big payoff is yours! These are the simple habits of intensifying focus that achieve sweet success.

Social networks of all sorts enhance staying on task. And we like it! Conformists thrive on working with other people to synergize efforts. Intensifying focus is simply shifted to the group effort. Excellent habits and the rewards of achievement now have a group, cooperative playing field.

Intensifying focus is one way of seeing, of seeing with the eye of the mind. It is the eye of planning, of logic, of the scientific. In focusing the eye of the heart, you look to ways of belonging, of nurturing, of bonding, of attuning to others.

There are other ways of seeing as well. There is also the eye of the soul. It is open to entirely new ways of perceiving and expressing, open to being inspired and integrating many modes of being, in distinctive, creative ways. The eye of the Spirit opens to pure being, with an aware, open and interconnected focus.

Your skills at intensifying focus and staying on task, will serve you well, no matter what other eye you open, no matter where you are in the spiral of life.

50 Conformist Relationships
Cooperative

A shared space of feeling, behavior and communication that we call relationship is a powerful thing. Yet most people meet routinely and superficially. Most relationships are unconscious, shaped by instinct, emotion and cultural learning. The connections may feel normal, usually a mix of tension and ease. In many relationships there is an unspoken leader, setting the tone, and then the one who responds or cooperates. These relationship patterns are often referred to as "the games people play." The patterns of these games become more obvious as we become more genuine and mature. The games melt when we interconnect openly and spontaneously and lovingly.

Conformist relationships are about social cooperation, getting along and having the joys of friendship, love and teamwork. Cooperation may seem like a blessing or a curse, depending on how conscious you are of what is going on, and what kind of games are in play, and who is setting the patterns. But no matter. You can always choose a healthy connection. How?

First, understand the nature of relating. Forget powerfully imposing your point of view on others. Yes, you may know better. You may not be understood, or you may be ignored or abused. Cooperative relationships are not just about you. Relating is about sharing a space with another. You need to express yourself. You aren't the whole show.

Second, pay attention to the other. In cooperative relationships you need to know where the other is coming from. Take in what's going on. Your take may not be quite right. Getting it right takes a lot of social intelligence and a lot of practice. Give it your best try.

Third, mirror what's going on. Share your take on things; simply say what you think is happening. To mirror, say things like, I hear you saying . . ., or It seems to me that . . ., or You mean . . . . It gives you a chance to do a reality check to see if you got it right. It gives the other person the pleasure of being correctly understood, and saying, "That's right." Or there can be a clarification. You both get on the same page through mirroring. Now you have a solid basis to cooperate, be it in work or love.

Fourth, respect the kind of relationship you are in. Is it work, friendship or intimate love? Don't confuse them. Each role is a pattern. Each role has its own rules. Relationships work when roles are clear and rules are followed. Under most circumstances, don't expect friendship from your employer. Don't work your friends.

Fourth, compromise. To get along, go along. Give a little to get a little. Yes, this can be done in a healthy way. Do not compromise on what matters most to you. Give a little where you can.

Finally, if something feels wrong, you may need the courage to speak up or change the way you are relating. Cooperation can slip into entangled, co-dependency patterns if you don't set limits. The difference between needy and cooperative is good self-care. An effective pattern in talking it out, is to use "I" statements, beginning a sentence with "I." "I" statements are not as threatening as "You" statements, which may sound judgmental and put your listener on the defensive. Using a mutually agreed upon signal, such as holding and passing a "talking stick," indicating that you have made your point and the other may respond, creates some safety in talking about difficult matters without fear of interruption.

If a relationship works and you can cooperate together, you will be happy. If you are not happy, something about the pattern is not right for you. Maybe it is unhealthy, showing responder patterns and these patterns need to change. Maybe the relationship is over or you are outgrowing the relationship, and it now feels suffocating. It is always risky, of course, to change. Yet your heart's desire is always to be free, no matter where you are in the spiral of life.

51 Conformist Emotions
Self Control

Emotions. They are your feelings, passions and longings. They are smart, natural, useful and instinctive guides, evaluating a situation faster than you can think and providing an instant response to changing circumstances. The needy and naïve have little control of their feelings. Acting on emotions in life and death situations may save your life. Acting on raw emotions in society may make you a loser. Social success requires self-control in expressing your emotions for the sake of cooperation and belonging. This may seem unfair and stifling, yet your social success depends on it.

Group success assumes and depends on the personal self-control of each individual. We all like people who are polite, show good manners, make us feel comfortable, and include us in group activities. We don't want to feel threatened by suspicion, emotional outbreaks or emotional neediness. Archie Bunker told Edith to stifle herself. John Kennedy said that class is grace under pressure. Either way, both express that controlling your emotions is highly desired.

How do you practice self-control when you find your emotions running high? Maybe a little lesson in brain structure will help. The emotional brain is part of the primitive brain, protecting you from perceived threat, by providing an instant response. It is at the base of the brain, while the thinking brain, in the forehead, takes a little time and evaluates what is going on before acting. This thinking helps the emotional, instinctive brain cool down, and so gives you control of your powerful emotions.

So, in times of strong emotions, especially anger, it is a good idea to cool down, count to ten, think before you speak, etc. These are all examples of thinking, of reflection, that create a cooling down of emotions. Thinking creates a temporary disconnect of the emotional brain from the thinking brain. Without reflection the emotional brain floods the whole brain. In cooling down, you get control of otherwise very overpowering feelings.

Anger is the most difficult emotion to manage, because it is usually fueled by self-righteousness. Anger is helped by a cool down. Humor also helps. So does compassion for the very one you are angry at. Both humor and compassion also require that you reflect in some way, and so get some distance on your powerful feelings.

Likewise, talking soothes traumatic emotions. Talking creates the disconnect from the emotional brain, because talking runs emotions through the thinking brain, and that cools down the emotions. Talking is the basis of success in talk therapy or of talking things out with a friend.

The recently popular idea that you should "let it all hang out" in public is seen now as primitive and naïve. Better to think of self-control in emotions as you being in charge and not your emotions. You express emotions with self-control by expressing the thoughtful, cooled-down version. You express your emotions when they are at simmer, not full boil. You are in charge, not your emotions.

Society's strong need for conformity has a down side. It can be stifling, with people often managing feelings by burying them. Getting on with the demands of the outer world represses a lot of personal sensitivity and expression. All this squelching of personal instinct works for many for a lifetime. This repression doesn't work for a lifetime for everyone. Some come to a point where personal stifling leads to personal pain. Depression may be the first symptom of repression. Or it may be anxiety, confusion or no longer getting along with people. All these emotions become signals that something needs to change.

Emotional pain motivates risk-taking with your feelings, opening up the Pandora's box and seeing what's in there. Thus begins the new adventure of learning to recognize emotions by naming them and expressing them appropriately. Thus, you are identifying and expressing emotions, with tact, and not merely holding back. Maintaining personal well-being, even in the midst of strong emotions, is the ultimate in emotional maturity. In this emotional maturity, you may find unexpected personal freedom and satisfaction.

52 Conformist Ethics
Reward and Punishment

What's right and what's wrong in personal choices is a huge question for every individual. Ethics is a code of right behavior that guides personal choices, leading to self-control, self-awareness and social conscience. This right behavior serves as the very basis for personal development, freedom and spiritual deepening. Without it, we cannot rise to our very best.

Society has a huge investment in a code of right behavior that guides personal self-control. Culture and civilization are based on a group consensus of preferred behavior. So from early on, you learn what is right and wrong from others. What is right and wrong is strongly encouraged by reward and punishment, the carrot and the stick. This right behavior serves society's need for control. These rewards and punishments reinforce law and order. Right behavior also leads to the joys of living together in work and love.

We learn right and wrong throughout our life. Some codes apply to less important things of socially acceptable ways of doing daily routines and are usually called social mores. Some codes apply to the more important issues of fairness to others and are called ethics.

The first teachers of right and wrong are in the home. Something is right to do if mom and dad approve. Something is wrong or bad if parents don't approve. Add to the mix, teachers, extended family, neighbors, media, and, finally, the law. In society, you will often pay to the last penny, if you are in trouble with the law. In turn, you will be rewarded with approval and the blessings of being cooperative, if you abide by the codes of your culture. When you are an adult, ethics codes become more sophisticated, with applications in professional standards and business ethics, as well.

Religious traditions often have elaborate codes of right and wrong behavior, with rewards for virtue, and punishment for transgressions. Some religions teach there is a God who sees all, who rewards the good and punishes the evil. Others rely on the natural law, written in the human heart, for a basis of right behavior.

Codes of right and wrong have variations to them, depending on the family and religion in which you are raised, the school you attend, the communities you grow up in. Only gradually do individuals see that there are different strokes for different folks.

It is only with much soul searching that individuals come into their own on moral values. They take the natural law, written in the human heart, and the outer, social codes, and come to their own conclusion on how to live, living by an internal standard of integrity. This is often scary for more traditional thinkers, who fear that choice means anything goes. Yet personal choice is at the very core of human dignity. The natural law is written in the heart of every one. Mature ethics is a responsible ethics. Ultimately fully developed personal ethics stops making choices with double standards and with personal gain in mind. The highest ethical standards lead to a universal standard, practicing universal compassion, justice and loving service.

53 Conformist Awareness
The Eyes Of Mind & Heart

Developing awareness of mind and heart into a successful, cooperative adult life takes some doing. It takes the human brain about twenty-five years to be fully mature. It is in your best interest and society's that you develop doing and belonging to the adult level of your society. You are then prepared to be a full participant in the game of life.

Your awareness for the eye of the mind, the thinking side of you, is, as a conformist, well aware of how society does things. This masculine or achieving side of life has grown through the hours, days, months and years that you spent in family, church, schools, on even on the street.

At some point you may, with your now more keenly developed logic, begin to see what might seem like a sneaky conspiracy. You may see that there seems to be a deep agreement among various social structures about how to do life. They seem to reinforce each other. Your family wants you to be successful. They urge good grades at school. School gets you ready for work. Work fires the economic engines. Politics often governs in favor of business. Religion urges respect for political authority.

Sure there is lip service given to being yourself, but always within the confines of the social norm. You become aware that there is enormous satisfaction in developing your abilities. You also learn just how far you can go. You quickly get negative feedback if you have stepped beyond what is acceptable, both in thinking and behavior.

The eye of heart is also now well developed. You are skilled at tuning into others' reality. Belonging has you seeking where and with whom you belong. You become aware that there are places and people and ideas that you love more than others, and some that actually repel you. Consider all the things chosen from the heart: friends, homes, music, interests, special knowledges, hobbies, clothing, cars, geography, animals, city vs. country, big company vs. little company, business vs. human service, the arts or conventional religion, etc. There's a place for you in all these choices.

A major dilemma in maturely living with both mind and heart is that mind and heart often have conflicting standards. As Pascal said, *The heart has its reasons that reason does not know.* Your mind may tell you that something is bad for you. Your heart may tell you that it's good for you. Yet awareness of this basic conflict between mind and heart is mostly nonexistent for conformists. Why? Because you can't afford to deal with such dilemmas, as you raise a family, make a living and keep up with the social demands of your group.

So, the mind/heart conflict is mostly outside of your awareness. The dilemmas are solved for you by society's "common sense," known through advice columns, self-help books, songs and movies, religious traditions, and when necessary, the law. The resolutions often reflect conventional wisdom. These will seldom give you your own highly individual resolution of such matters.

So conformist mind/heart awareness is well developed for your success in society. As conventional answers start feeling like,

"Been there, done that," you may find yourself seeking an awareness that is more finely tuned to you, personally. You demand something more genuine for yourself, deeper, richer, more soul satisfying. Mind and heart move to a deeper, more reflective level. Your companions become your own yearnings, fantasies, imagination, dreams and even nature. The realms of self-help may beckon, or philosophy, religion, transpersonal psychology, holistic science, poetry, mythology and other cultures. This seeking may ultimately lead you to the very source of your deeper self, the realm of Spirit and Being, vast, rich and free.

54 Conformist Wisdom
To Conventional Answers

Wisdom provides answers to life's most difficult issues. There is suffering, illness, pain, loss and death. When these realities break into our well-run lives of doing and belonging, of being good and everything will be OK, except it isn't, we seek ways to make sense of the senseless. We seek answers. What are we supposed to do, in our pain?

If you look to yourself, you may find that you have your own ways of dealing with suffering. It might be avoidance, not thinking about it or distracting yourself. It may be denial, assuring yourself that nothing is wrong. Staying busy and letting time heal actually may be a helpful way to cope, for some. Or, like a wounded animal, we may seclude ourselves in times of pain, trusting the healing power from within to take its course.

Looking outside oneself for relief and solace is also immensely helpful. Family, friends and the larger community show support when we are in need, opening their hearts. You feel strong, unsuspected gratitude for the simplest favors. Being on the receiving end of genuine support and empathy in times of crisis opens your heart as well.

Where we go for wisdom varies. Some go within themselves and try to figure things out. Others read. For some it is a friend, a parent or a teacher. Others go to a church advisor. Some find a professional therapist. Self-help groups, such as AA, can be very successful, where healing is helped by the simple act of connecting with others, speaking openly and being heard by non-judgmental and compassionate fellow human beings.

Religious groups provide time honored ways of wisdom. Religious leaders, schooled in their given traditions, often can provide needed and welcomed and trusted answers to suffering. Their insights and compassion may resonate with the wisdom written in your own heart. These traditional answers often comfort.

We humans often cry out to God in our suffering, even if we are nonbelievers. We seek release from our suffering, somehow hoping, instinctively, that relief exists, even as we feel utterly forlorn and helpless and disbelieving. That there is a place of relief and solace is at the core of our wailing. The God you cry out to is seen as a responsive God, a Father God, one who knows, who cares, and who responds to your pleas for relief.

But what if your suffering continues? Losses multiply. Death is coming. You find no comfort in the traditional answers given you. Everything given you is meaningless. You grow bitter with pain and hopelessness. Then what?

Humans cannot live without meaning, without making sense of things. Your crisis of meaning throws you out of life as you knew it, into a wilderness, where you are without comfort or protection. Your crisis of meaning is also the beginning of your journey to find something unchangeable, rock solid. It may not come to you through the conventional channels any longer or you may need to make them your own. You are instinctively impelled to find your own meaning, your own answers to life's most difficult questions.

You may not find comfort in conventional answers, and instead become stoic and face things as they are, and simply "deal with things." Or you may despair and fall into deepest depression and hopelessness. Yet life goes on, even in you, despite your inconsolable suffering. Life keeps on giving its gifts. In the deeper realms of your being, despite outward suffering, you may find the paradox of unexpected personal peace. Perhaps suffering has softened you and opened your heart. This healing place within is beyond time's conditioning, opening your heart to your spirit home, where there is no suffering. Here we know, when we arrive, that we have found where we have always belonged.

Conformist Social Development

55 Conformist Family
Family of Origin, Committed Relationships and Support Circles

The human urge for kinship seems to be relentless. We deeply need to belong, to live together, to function within a group, to feel shared connections, to know and be known. We crave community, children, physical and emotional security and mutual support. And we experience pleasure in both giving and receiving, in providing help in time of need, encouragement in time of difficulty, and also in receiving recognition in times of success. It is only in the context of committed relationships that children can grow strong, individuals feel secure in their vulnerability, and members of a given community find a home for their shared worldview.

Tolstoy wrote that all happy families are happy in the same way, while unhappy families are unhappy in different ways. The conventional family is probably close to Tolstoy's sense of happy.

What is that conventional sense of happy? Something like this. A man and a woman meet, each feeling that they have met someone special. Such is the magic of intimate partnership, of being in love. They marry and live happily ever after. They have kids, create an ideal childhood for their kids that they can remember as a happy childhood. It is the home with the white picket fence around it. The kids grow up, find their true work, fall in love and have kids of their own. The generations stay close.

A man and woman may look to marry well, choosing a partner who enhances their social and financial status. "Marrying up" may be for looks, smarts, achievements, possessions, social standing or connections. Simply getting married gives you status and recognition in the community. It is a great achievement, part of the successful, good life.

Men and women have traditional marriage values when looking for desirable qualities in the other. A man looks for a woman who will be an agreeable spouse, supportive of his career, a good mother to his kids, a good homemaker, and attractive to his friends. A woman's traditional values look to a man who will love her, be a good provider financially, be a virile, healthy and handsome father for her children, and who values fidelity and family life. Stereotype? Yes, indeed. This is the conformist pattern.

Healthy family life generates win/win emotional security. You feel you matter, are cared about and belong. There is synergy, the strength that one and one are more than two. It's encouraging to have your family members' support and have them recognize your achievements in the bigger world of school, work and love.

Cooperating and working out problems is simply smart. Your family is a place to learn these skills. And it's OK to ask for help, and give support as you can. Family is deeply tied to traditional values of caring, of conforming, of doing and belonging. You are encouraged to live by the rules of society and play your roles as best you can.

It is a genuine crisis for any individual to change and find himself or herself different from the family's conventional patterns. To recognize your differences, to be true to your individuality, means you must find a new way of doing family. It must be more genuine for you. It becomes the daunting, but vital challenge of your family

Kathy Kouzmanoff

living to be inclusive of differences. Ultimately, this extends to the universal family of man.

56 Conformist Politics
Personal Rights, Public Good, Public Safety and Public Office

Politics is a dance, a continuous struggle, between the personal rights and power of individuals and the rights and power of authority over them. The struggle is as old as civilization itself. It varies from brutal to manipulative to idealistic. Politics is a profession of governing, with practitioners taking various positions in balancing personal interest and the greater public good.

You can be in a political party that is liberal and favors more social support and government protections for people. You can be a conservative and favor less government and less support for individuals, encouraging rugged individualism. Whichever is your preference, as a conformist, you use power well, and are savvy, smart and successful in using it.

In democratic countries, where the rights of the individual are the basis of elected government, it is the ideal to protect universal rights and set limits on extremism of any kind. Schools are funded; government has a system of checks and balances and is mostly free of corruption. There is economic opportunity for anyone to get ahead. There is freedom of religion. Taxes are used for the public good. Political power is used to strengthen stability and opportunity for individuals to flourish.

In countries without a healthy democracy, and there are many, the norm is not tilted in favor of individual rights, but in favor of strong, often corrupt power. There is little political or religious freedom. There is poor education, and uneven or nonexistent economic opportunity.

A good politician in a democratic country is a savvy team player, championing his or her party's interests and inspiring the masses to join and get involved. Actions are carefully calculated, sometimes ten or twenty years ahead, to shape public opinion, to literally change the way the public perceives a given action. Black may be called white and white black. Parties never admit to such duplicity, but point it out eagerly in the opposition.

Volunteering in a political campaign is a good way to be active in your political beliefs. If you believe in a cause, you want to work for it and make a contribution. You want to be a doer, not just a talker.

Your interest in politics goes beyond your own personal needs. You seek to support law and order, stability and opportunity. Your keen appreciation of group life seeks to protect both individual rights and the common good. Domestic and foreign peace gives people a basis to prosper, without fear of violence or unfavorable economic regulations.

Your political style is even-handed and pragmatic. Criminals should be punished for their misdeeds and pay their price to society. Government needs to protect its citizens and uphold the law. Welfare and other safety nets are needed for society's helpless and needy, but may or may not be there, as individualism and the social good become unbalanced.

Politics can run amok, as well. Power can become manipulative, devious, heartless and corrupt. Ignorance and intolerance of differences can violate human dignity. So do lack of equal opportunity, lawlessness, greed, lies, cover-up and incompetence.

All of these beg for caring individuals to get involved. Your actions show your values. It is not what you say, but what you do, and why, that matter. The art of the possible, that is politics, has conformists doing the work necessary to bring your values into reality.

57 Conformist Religion/Arts
Art, Philosophy, Psychology and Religion

Conformist traditions are those most widely held in the culture. Their interpretation of how to live well becomes institutionalized in systems of education, family and religious authority. To the majority of individuals, these systems are seen as the norm and are devotedly learned and passed on, often without much questioning.

The values usually mirror and reinforce the needs of growing up as a person, being productive in the workplace, conforming to the laws of government and fitting into human society. Hence, cooperation is stressed, as is belonging, achievement, fairness and respect for authority.

Likewise, the art or aesthetic taste of conformists tends toward the traditional and widely acceptable. As an art student, you dutifully learn the tradition and skills of your medium. It is often readily understood and non-controversial. It evokes the familiar, be it in emotions, aesthetic style or commemoration of historic persons and events.

The blessings of belonging to a group supporting personal values and growth are especially rich. The group provides the deep joys of caring kinship. Your religious community supports you as none other can, with its members devoted to caring for their own, with understanding and generosity. In addition, the group provides answers from its traditions to your search for meaning, especially in times of loss, grief, illness, suffering, old age and death. Your community provides a lifelong structure for you to deal with the ups and downs that life inevitably brings.

In addition, the values of your tradition are ones you deeply cherish and try to live by and pass on to your children and the wider community. You know that you are beneficiary of the generations who have gone before, and the values are tried and true. In many cases, you know that you are standing on the shoulders of giants.

Your personal values provide you with a strong personal identity. You defend your standards vigorously. You take justifiable pride in your good works and accomplishments. These good works bring you the admiration and recognition of others. Not only are you a valuable community member. Your community appreciates and recognizes your smart and successful accomplishments.

The God of conventional Christianity may reward the good and punish the wicked, but the Judeo/Christian/Muslim God is also a caring and merciful God. He provides for your needs, and knows of them before you even ask. He is your Heavenly Father, after all. This God may be relied upon. God is also male, with devoted, female figures surrounding Him. These Christian females may be venerable, but they are not divine. Likewise, patriarchal values of authority and hierarchy are dominant, with its sacred rituals seen as the primary means of grace.

As long as you find these socially bound traditions enlivening for you, they continue to keep your values strong. When bad things happen to good people, through these very institutions, you may experience a crisis of faith. There may be financial or sexual scandal, or personal betrayal. There may be anger, confusion, power plays and even rejection. Standards that once worked, interpretations that once meant everything, now seem corrupt with power, small-minded and stifling. Respecting authority looks like passivity and naïve childishness.

You no longer feel respect or that you belong. You may feel impelled to set out into a scary unknown, free of the group that once sustained you. The quest demands that you to be more self reliant, more honest with yourself and more expressive to others of your own truth than you ever thought possible. Your own self-awareness and well-being guide you now, to what matters most.

58 Conformist Sex/Closeness
Eroticism, Sex, Connectedness, Love, Communication, Masculine and Feminine Orientation

For the conformist, connectedness takes a gigantic leap from mere self-centeredness and self-indulgence. Good connecting, good conversation and good sex now find delight, completion and joy in an actual relationship, where there is a shared space of relating, of sharing, respect, and not mere self interest. Both partners actually take pleasure in the benefits of self-control and emotional intelligence, experiencing the joys of cooperation, feeling safe, understood, accepted and heard.

Conversations are warm and appropriate. Sexual morality is deeply shaped by community standards of commonly accepted mores, church teachings and the law. Sexual fantasies are romantic, about your regular partner, or used to enhance your sexual relationship with your regular partner. Child pornography is unthinkable. Fidelity to one partner is the conventional norm. Sexual discrimination laws both define and protect personal sexual dignity. Social harmony depends on the strict adherence to these codes. Stable relationships strengthen our sense of self, providing belonging, family, home, social status, security and stability.

Yet conventional love and connectedness are full of hopeless contradictions, leading to all sorts of confusions and schemes in the name of love. On the one hand conformist love is hopelessly naïve and romantic, seeking our completion in the perfection we see in another. On the other hand conformist love can be utterly practical,

143

sizing up the other for social advantage or personal gain. This is a steely-eyed view of love, indeed.

Our cultural norm of romantic love is actually a rare and awesome experience, exciting, idealistic, glamorous, intense and tender, all at once. Yet, this romantic love, so charged with energy, can be illusory too, part need, part fantasy and part projection. Because it is the culturally accepted ideal of what "real" love is, in large parts of the world, we take for granted that only romantic love is the real thing. We are often unprepared when the illusion gets tarnished.

We may experience poor communication, lack of cooperation, betrayal or abuse. It is at this point that many people begin to re-live the wounding and sense of powerlessness that marked their childhood, including fears of abandonment. Vague and nameless fears arise. Romantic love is unraveling and it is hard to know how to handle the pain and loss of love. Repressing the pain, or trying to fix things through more love often seems to be the way to cope. But, in the end, this probably just intensifies one's problems.

Double standards may also abound, as individuals try to reconcile a failing romance and their own childhood needs all at once. You may be adept at making good impressions, using your cunning to say one thing, yet do another. Conventional moral codes may be ignored. There may be lies, affairs and destructive psychological games. This lack of integrity, which seems so worldly wise, so necessary for emotional survival when love fails, leads to your own cynicism. You really don't believe in goodness, morality or the sincerity of others anymore.

So, does loss of romantic love mean that love is an illusion, that it's all just fantasy? Some do indeed come to that conclusion. Others may transform their loving into something stronger, where relating is about honesty, trust, sharing, listening and a real commitment to understand and grow together. This sharing and listening creates a safe companionship of true intimacy. Even the negative or the unacceptable can be shared, sometimes with humor, but always with candor and compassion. Authentic intimacy creates a matrix, a source of ongoing mutual self-exploration, expression, acceptance and growth in freedom. Eventually the deepening connection may extend the circle of love, widening it to all.

59 Conformist Social Situations
Food, Shelter, Clothing, Cyberspace, Society and Time

Look around you and see what most people are doing, how they
live, what they think and how they love. This is the conformist
level of society. Observe how children learn, how shared
background bonds people to their traditions, be it class and money,
culture, nationality, family or religion. Note how natural resources
are used, how they affect lifestyle and politics. Note how the media
mirrors and even deepens what most people do and value. Note
what is considered healthy or acceptable and what is considered
unacceptable, out of the norm, or even "sick."

You too have learned the codes of your group in order to be
successful socially, to be fashionable, to be right for promotion at
work. Any lack of success is a failure to conform. This conformity
touches everything: what to believe, where to get an education,
your place of work, the use of alcohol, health care standards, drug
use, choosing clothes, cars, homes, furnishings, pets, foods, sports,
hobbies and politics.

Capitalism encourages constant change in what you own and what
you do. Throw out the old. Bring in the new. Do worry about the
future, about having enough, about a good retirement. Keep
working for a worry-free future. Personal desire is controlled only
by what you can afford and by the law. Opportunists, however,
delight in getting "something for nothing." They are often folk
heroes to others, seen as those who defied the system. These
double standards, where practiced, quickly lead to cynicism and
social alienation. Simplicity, regard for things old, being frugal or

practicing self-denial for the greater good, are not valued in a consumer society.

The individual's maintaining a proper appearance, being well-mannered, cooperative and respectful, all contribute to the overall soundness of any society, to making it "work" and also making the individual successful within it. Does this amount to wearing a mask? Yes, often it does. Under this social mask there may be a person with the inner liberty to lead a more complex personal life.

Society's institutions are brilliant at reinforcing the status quo. Consider how banking encourages debt, advertising encourages need, and government establishes policies to maintain and regulate it all. In the days of settling the far open lands of the United States, the government gave free land to settlers, industry designed farm machinery not before needed, advertising promoted such mechanized farming, and banks lent the money to buy the expensive machinery. A mule and forty acres would no longer be enough for the good life. How often have you heard your schooling connected to future financial reward, and not to personal satisfaction or the growth of your soul?

As a conformist, you do what most people do and you do it well. Yet, in every group there will always be the restless ones, the visionaries, the seekers, the ones who ask, Is that all there is? They feel like they are waking up to a broader way of living. These bold individuals hear a different drummer, and are relentless in often going it alone, breaking out of the norm, often at the cost of great personal pain and loneliness. To others they may look foolish, demented or just plain weird. Yet, this is exactly how individuals, groups, and eventually whole societies, move forward. We live with the hope that such change is transforming us toward greater connectedness, freedom, knowledge, justice and love.

60 Conformist Work
Money, Livelihood, Hobbies, Special Interests, Daily Routines and Useful Activity

If anything represents conformist work, it is western capitalism. It is lifestyle, value system and worldview all rolled into one. You think, eat and sleep work. If you play this game well, you are the epitome of intelligence and success and are usually handsomely rewarded.

The streets of America were said to be paved with gold for immigrants, and on the force of this dream, many came here, and still do, to make their fortunes. Horatio Alger's stories live. Poor boy practices self-discipline, courage and hard work and gets a good life. Hard working blue collar and middle class Americans today often dream bigger dreams today than the protagonists of Alger's stories, wanting more than merely doing OK. They dream of great wealth, perhaps subconsciously identifying with the very rich! So it seems, as many ordinary folk literally vote away their own best interests in public social programs, siding with the interests of the rich, rather than their own.

The encouragement to dream and succeed is heard in these common phrases: 'Nothing succeeds like success!' 'Dream big.' 'If you can think it, you can do it!' 'The difficult we do immediately, the impossible takes a little longer!' And, 'If you build it, they will come.' Such attitudes stoke the fires of ambition and drive us to work hard, and even to gamble and take on enormous debt in the hope of future rewards.

The drive for success may bring out your personal best. The challenge to do well, belong to a larger vision and meet exacting standards can generate enormous pride and personal satisfaction in a job well done. In addition, success brings with it good income, status and a sense of belonging and recognition. Stress and pressure? Maybe. Probably. Rome wasn't built in a day. When the going gets tough, the tough get going.

You are also a good team player. Work demands a trustworthy character. You do your part, holding up high standards, being reliable, and playing by the rules. You know just how far you can bend the rules without getting into trouble or being inappropriate.

Being organized and productive demands clear thinking from you. You know your goals and manage your time. You have the personal discipline to stay on task. You are rarely caught short of money or time. You focus on the important, and know how to break it down into smaller, achievable tasks.

A competitive spirit motivates you as well, with you measuring your success against others. You know there is stiff competition out there, and you may need to work, work, work and even step over other people on the way to the top. Getting ahead is the name of the game. You don't change jobs unless you can advance your career, make more money, get more prestige, more perks, better working conditions, a better fit or more security. Even outside of work, you may use contacts to get ahead, to see and be seen, to be in the right place at the right time.

Success requires knowing how to create win/win situations. You respect people, making them feel important and heard. Your attitude generates loyalty and return customers.

Support is everywhere to be smart, savvy and successful. It keeps the social engine running. However, when work seems to be getting routine, depressing, boring, mechanized, alienating, change is knocking. The suppressed dreams you've tucked away in your heart may get stronger. Doing something great, perhaps with greater self-expression, beckons. Maybe it's doing something less for money, and more for creativity, for something you love, or for public service. The conformist norm begins to lose its grip on you. More personally inspired visions insist on being taken seriously. Depression and boredom may be doors, acting as invitations to more demanding, more fulfilling and more self-actualizing work. Inspiration leads, where once conformity reigned.

Level 3   Individualist

Individualist Basics

Receptive, Reflective And Real

Soul

(Ego and Self)

Basic Task: To Reflect And Get Real
Basic Value: Authenticity
Basic Belief: If I Am Myself, I Will Be Fulfilled.
Basic Problem: I Am Myself And Something Is Missing.
Motto: *I Gotta Be Me.* OR *To thine own self be true, and thou canst not be false to any other.*

61 Individualist Description
Receptive, Reflective and Real (Soul)

Some things you were conditioned to do and believe still work for you as an individualist, and others don't. Individualist changes often occur in one's mid-30's to mid-50's, although there can be breakthroughs at any time. You notice that you aren't so willing to go along with how things are. You need to be more reflective and more genuine in your self-awareness and self-expression. You feel like you are "waking up."

Such times are often periods of great inner turmoil. Increasing dissatisfaction with the outer world often marks them. We sometimes feel that we are losing our way and in need of a lot of soul searching, withdrawing from the world, studying or just trying new things.

Ideally, we don't spiral backward and regress to the level of the responder under the stress of personal change. Awareness of others hopefully is still a mark of our character, as we continue to build on all the doing and belonging skills that are already in place.

However, old friends and interests often no longer hold our attention as they once did. They may seem too bound by convention, or lacking in insight. By contrast, you seem more able to face more things head on. You seem to have more courage to talk about things that others may want to ignore. Self-discovery, self-expression and self-actualization are now of paramount importance. Yet, those around you may be confused and angered by your behaviors. In fact, they may feel that they don't understand you any longer. Nor do they know how to relate to you.

In psychological terms, you are still mostly productive and not stagnant, yet this activity may also entail periods of withdrawal, as you deal with confusion, doubt and change. Religious identity also becomes a more personal matter, as it reflects your own inner experience and deepening knowing.

Humor may be aimed at yourself, as you find your way, or aimed at seekers and dreamers of all sorts. It may also have a darker side, a kind of M A S H humor, used to get through unavoidable personal misery.

The individualist's shadow side may show in reverting back to selfishness, with little outer involvement or concerns for others. You might confuse license with maturing freedom. You may become confused, even overwhelmed, as you attempt to integrate more subtle and conflicting parts of yourself into your identity. Profound emotional and psychological changes may create crises in your relationships, and in your personal, physical and mental health.

Responders sometimes think that individualists are just like them. That is, they may confuse self-centeredness with maturing self-expression. Conformists may be irritated with individualists, since they are seen as breaking out of the confines of the norm, and they are hard to understand and are resented for changing.

Those at the conscient level have the wisdom to see that you are waking up and they are often pleased. You are in the process of shedding unconscious conditioning and integrating new freedom, inspiration and passion into your life. The conscient also realizes that inflation and grandiosity are a temptation for the individualist.

Individualists show a receptive, reflective and real face when they are assessed in relation to common personality traits or preferences. Personality preferences between personality opposites, as listed below, (the preferences used in a widely used personality indicator[16]), can all have an individualist level of development, as suggested here.

The individualist *introvert* values self-examination, personal honesty, inner depth and meaning. The *extravert* is energized by personalized self-expression that is creative, subtle and genuine.

The *sensing type* masters different ways of perceiving and integrates them. The *intuitive type* gives intuition serious consideration as another way of knowing.

The *thinking type* understands the logic of differing realities, each having their own ways of knowing. The *feeling type* consciously names emotions and learns from them, all of them, but does not necessarily act upon them.

The *ordering type* (or *judger*) integrates goals and time management with larger goals, like lifetime or personal mission goals. The *go with the flow type* (or *perceiver*) organizes by consciously following personal rhythms that integrate complexity and that satisfy.

Some basic personality traits that are often viewed as indicators of a healthy personality can show individualist level development.

Emotional stability is fluid. Your emotions are observed, named and integrated into your life overall. Some are expressed. Some are not.

Agreeableness is richly layered, being gracious, generous and genuine. You can integrate manners with candor, which makes you both diplomatic and trustworthy.

Reliability is both respectful and candid.

Openness to change or experience is highly prized. You are open to new horizons and self-discovery, and to the means to explore them.

62 Individualist Basic Task
To Reflect and Get Real

Your basic task as an individualist is to step back from your old ways of believing, behaving and relating, and try to get some personal perspective on how things are. You are living less out of prior conditioning, and more out of personal reflection. You can stand back from your own experiences and are an observer to your own experiences, past and present.

You look at yourself to get more insight on who you really are and why you act the way you do. You ponder what you really want from life. You look at your relationships and your work. You become more realistic and honest about what is right for you and what isn't. You consider new ways of relating, doing and believing. There is more to you than society says is the norm. You are more complex, contradictory and even insightful. You are more and more aware of your own unique, specially gifted self.

You are more open to emotional experiences as well, since you are able to acknowledge issues and feelings that may have been repressed in yourself and projected onto others. This is possible because you are able to take a look at things with more personal freedom, as you can now practice the role of an observer. As observer, you are curious, but you don't condemn. You simply practice being reflective, receptive and real.

63 Individualist Basic Value
Authenticity

You have an inner urgency as an individualist to be true to who you really are, and not just to go along with others' ways of seeing and doing things. You most value authenticity.

In the realm of action, authenticity is about right work. Competence and accomplishment are no longer enough. There is now an issue of what you really care about, in work, and what really expresses you. It is no longer enough just to work for the sake of working or making money.

In the world of belonging, authenticity is about right relating. You look at who you are with and how and why. Some relationships are for life and cannot be changed, such as childhood home, schools, family and special friends. Other relationships have more flexibility, such as chosen friendships, homes and extended family.

In both areas, how you relate becomes more expressive of your individual self.

Doing and belonging in an honest and accountable way becomes the focus for individualists. Individualists realize that you are responsible, as the Little Prince said, for what they have tamed. Your own self-development insists on living this ever-changing cultivation that is your life with more and more personal authenticity.

64 Individualist Basic Belief
If I Am Myself, I Will Be Fulfilled

Everything in you as an individualist is urging you to greater self-awareness and self-actualization. It leads you to make the changes that seem necessary to stretch your boundaries.

You are aware you are capable of so much more than your daily life gave expression to in the past. The constraints of everyday life often seem severe now, so much so, that you may feel trapped, almost as though there is no exit.

You realize that you must make changes. You must become who you are and do what you really want. You must "follow your bliss,"[17] take your journey, do your thing, be yourself. You aim to discover yourself, to grow, to change, to matter, to make a contribution that is distinctively yours.

Being yourself can manifest itself in many ways, some of them quite conventional, such as travel, a new friend, a different church, moving, starting a new business, getting a divorce, going back to school, or simply being an adventurer.

Being yourself can also be done in more unconventional ways, such as being an artist or a spiritual seeker, joining people in service of a cause. Or you may make a truly unique contribution, forged with inspirations from your deepest Self.

Individualists often undergo enormous personal transformations. Joining a Twelve Step Program can, for example, change your life, as you receive unconditional love and learn to accept personal responsibility. Going into Jungian analysis, or experiencing a spiritual conversion, may hammer together your little self and big Self into a new indestructible you, which is beyond your imagining. You may find that these personal experiences help others, as well. You reinterpret traditional beliefs, giving modern expression to ancient truths, motivating wider commitments.

65 Individualist Basic Problem
I Am Myself and Something Is Missing

Becoming an individual and being true to yourself hopefully has served you well, bringing deep fulfillment. You have become self-actualized. You have done the work you were given by life to do. Now what?

Are you supposed to just keep seeking more and more new adventures, creating more and more self-expression, or devoting more of yourself to a worthy cause? What if one day, it all feels like, Been there, done that.

Having done what life asked of you, developing from responder to conformist to individualist, may now surprisingly lead you to a totally new and unexpected horizon. It may be the most boundless of your life. It is full of paradox, one that brings together seeming opposites, into a conscious and connected whole.

This new horizon is beyond all doing and belonging and self-actualizing. It is the realm of a more universal life, the life of a free, unbounded spirit. It is a realm of riches beyond measure. And its unbounded realm, full of paradox, is yours. There is rest within action, doing within being, stillness within knowing, joy within suffering, love within aversion.

If up to now you have trusted yourself for answers, consider this. Your yearnings within you for something beyond merely being yourself are the very witness within you that there is a life of the free, unbounded spirit.

66 Individualist Motto
I Gotta Be Me. To thine own self be true, and thou canst not be false to any other man.

I gotta be me.

Individuality is particularly prized in western culture and has been for almost one thousand years. We give the last vestige of our energy to self-determination, to self-reliance, to going it alone, if necessary.

Daring to try,

to do it or die,

I gotta be me.

This is the dramatic urgency that takes us over when our spirit rises up within us, unbidden, to self-actualize. No matter what the cost, we find ourselves impelled to leave the pack and strike out to find our own buried treasure.

To thine own self be true, and thou canst not be false to any other.

With these words Shakespeare urged personal integrity. If we compromise our deepest truth, we cannot relate to anyone well. It is muddled, and the other knows something is off, because we create confusion, rather than clarity, in them. With integrity, we can only be true to others, creating transparency and even joy. This personal integrity also leads you by instinct to know who are good companions for you.

Individualist Personal Development

67 Individualist Motivation
Individuality

The sweet thrill of success that you are somebody in the world and that you belong, no longer motivates. Self-realization and self-expression become urgent for the individualist. You are going deeper into yourself, finding out what you are really all about. Waking up, seeing things as they are and naming them accurately, become driving motivations.

Becoming an individual is a deeply solitary thing, and often lonely. You are not the first to go down this path, and not everyone does. Why one is called to wake up and another is not is truly mysterious.

Motivation toward a deeper you is often jump-started by a sudden crisis, loss or maybe something strenuous physically, like an accident, childbirth or even rigorous sports. Religious practices may open you. Others simply belong to the "grower's club," and can't get enough of self-discovery. Others seem to be motivated by midlife, demanding more than mere routines of the past. Others feel moved by something as vague as greatness. Some want to know their life's work and do it.

Who am I, really? Why do I feel the way I do? Why is nothing I do good enough? Why don't I have friends, fit in or belong? Why did I act that way? Why am I hurting? Why am I restless? How can I get free of the rat race? Where is our country going? Why am I having disturbing dreams and what do they mean? Why does life seem meaningless? How do I find meaning? How can I meaningfully contribute to the world, to my country, to the community?

You begin to realize that you are not a simple creature. You are pulled in many directions, often contradictory. Where does it all come from? You aren't happy to simply blame others any longer. You have to look to yourself. You see and accept, ever so slowly, your contradictions, your idiosyncrasies and your "shadow side." You experience urgent and vague yearnings, capable of shape-shifting you into a new and richer person than you ever dreamed.

The journey to integrate this complexity may take several different roads. Some look to logic, to philosophy, to science. Others look to the past of childhood. Some look to the present for more insight into recurring patterns. Still others interpret their dreams, seeing them as "the royal road to the unconscious," as Freud said. Jung saw dreams coming from a center in the psyche called the Self (with a capital "S"). It acts as a guide, often giving dreams to motivate, advise and heal.

Mythology can motivate, providing stories that are metaphors of the inner life, teaching about realities of the spirit that mere logic can't touch. Metaphysical schools of thought may appeal to you as well.

Religious traditions may also be attractive to you, whether for taking a new eye to those you are already familiar with, or for exploring another tradition, once unfamiliar, but now appealing.

This stretch toward depth, complexity, acceptance and integration often leads to something that is larger than your personal self, something that deeply satisfies. The depth generates universality in your sympathies. Through going within, you become more connected without. Greater playfulness, acceptance and love may result. The trickster god may also appear, with its wry sense of humor, poking fun at the self-delusion and foibles of being human.

Responders or conformists may see individualist motivation as a bit odd, eccentric and weird. No matter. You mix cooperation with individuality, as graciously as is your style. You accept that you have stepped out of the norm and may not be understood by others. You may or may not attempt to explain yourself to others. People appreciate if you do explain yourself, as it helps them to understand you better, and may encourage their own self-exploration as well.

You may find unexpected strength-giving energies available to you as you take yourself more seriously. This path may well lead you into full waking up and oneness with Being itself.

68 Individualist Identity
Authentic

Identity, who you think you are, how you know yourself, describe yourself, name yourself, is getting richer, more real, more genuine. You are not just a cooperative, nice person, successful in society. You also have complications and contradictions and a shadow side. You also sense that there is something more to you than your personal history and personal conditioning.

Being more authentic is a massive shift from merely conforming and being a good, acceptable, productive and predictably nice person. You still do all of that well, knowing that it's part of playing your part in day-to-day life.

But in your more private world, a more complex identity is emerging. It starts when you begin to want more from life than merely adapting and conforming to outer expectations and standards. The conformist box is just too small. You are restless and even depressed, but not knowing why. To relieve the pain, you start probing, trying to figure out what's going wrong.

It's like opening Pandora's box. You have to admit your dissatisfaction, your yearnings for something more. Life's not perfect and neither are you. You realize, with a sharp sting, the limitations of the life around you and within you. You look at the unlikable, even the forbidden. You may find that you share traits with the very people you despise. These glimpses into yourself and the life you live used to be shoved away. Now, however, you want to take a closer look. They may give you insight into what you are looking for.

How do people find the courage to look at what has been unacceptable for so long? Call it attitude or maybe mindfulness. You've found courage and freedom to take a kind of observer's point of view on all the complexity coming into focus. You are thoughtful, receptive, and not judgmental or defensive. Whatever you become aware of, you let it come in onto your inner radar screen. This means that you can take in what you receive, observe it, sit with it but do not get overwhelmed. You choose to act or not act. This is your freedom, allowing a richer, more interesting, more individual, more complicated, less defensive person to emerge. If you didn't have this personal inner freedom center to observe, but not act, you might simply once again act like a responder, subject to forces within and without. More mindful sitting with yourself is needed.

Your inner cast of contradictory impulses becomes familiar to you. You understand that they war against each other. Some try to cripple you with condemning judgment. Others are manic and expect too much. Others seem to beckon you into living a more selfless life, beyond mere personal self-interest, perhaps entirely unique to you.

You are relieved to learn that there is more to life than merely adapting and conforming to outer expectations and standards. You are not losing it if the norm of your culture doesn't turn you on anymore. Your identity is waking up, less repressed, more flexible, more open, more honest. Your newfound freedom may find you taking seriously impassioned inspirations to follow your own star.

You take pleasure in being freed from the far too little box of society's expectations and the compulsive demands of your own personal demons. Your personal identity now includes an inner freedom allowing for greater complexity and personal inspiration.

You actually begin to love this place of personal freedom, with its joy. This experience of personal freedom releases an immense feeling of liberation within. You recognize that this freedom reflects a more authentic, less conditioned sense of yourself.

69 Individualist Focus
Integrating

Focus, your ability to direct your attention, is becoming richer. No longer do you simply focus your attention on your chosen goals or discipline. You are beginning to integrate seemingly disconnected realities in your life, parts that before just seemed to be a jumble of contradictions, which seemed to make no sense at all.

You experience yourself standing as mediator between the outer world and your inner world. You experience both. Sometimes they seem to be amazingly different worlds. You find that you actually want to be a mediator, to bring these disparate worlds together. You find that you are consciously cooperation with something within you that already is creating coherence among your worlds, beyond your effort. This mysterious weaving is layered, complex, rich and satisfying.

As mediator between worlds, you have many eyes. You have the eye of body, protecting you physically and emotionally. You have the eye of mind, logic and achievement. You have the eye of heart, feeling and belonging. Now the eye of soul is opening. It is your inner eye, receptive, open to inspiration and the richness of inner realities. Somehow, in ways beyond the conscious mind, your soul begins to expand your sense of things and begins to make sense of your expanded experience. In some ways, being the mediator is also being the observer, the witness to many ways of experiencing reality.

This soul focus has new ways to integrate your life. You begin to sense a story that you are living. You see that your story helps you to understand yourself and the world. It may not be a story that you choose, but it starts putting the pieces together. Your story may even remind you of stories of other times and places. Knowing the story satisfies. You start to recognize the story by seeing yourself in literature, movies and others' experiences.

You see that your story creates insight and meaning. The story has patterns and symbols that give insight into your experience. The patterns and symbols of your story start to bring the outer and the inner worlds together. Philosophers may call this existentialism. Psychology may call it individuation or being authentic. Religion finds this the stuff of metaphysics, mythology or spirituality. Neurobiology sees it as the function of the prefrontal cortex of the brain, the seat of mindfulness. The brain acts as a storyteller, a great interweaver of all the various parts of your living.

Yet, despite all these traditions of personal knowing, how can you be sure of the meaning of your life, or where you are in the spiral of life? As with all things personal, you are the final judge of your own experience. Does your story ring true for you?

An especially powerful way of integrating inner and outer worlds is your nighttime dreams. Carl Jung thought they came from the center point of our psyches, the Self, and gave us compensation, balance and direction, especially if we work with them consciously. In working with dreams consciously, we are basically making associations with the various dream images, amplifying what comes to mind with the images. There is usually an "aha" inside us that signals a meaningful insight. Insight satisfies, and often leads to inspiration to act. If you take dreams as a kind of inner guidance or wisdom, you can integrate their insight into your life. Jungians call this process "individuation," this hammering together of the inner and the outer, the conscious and the unconscious.

Integrating the disconnected parts of your life into a story is something that we do over and over in our lives, little by little. The more we integrate, the richer the story and the more fascinating to listeners. This is the work of artists, of writers and of every one of us. We are all storytellers.

The symbols, that move us and by which we live, motivate us powerfully, be they from the media, family, government, pop culture, religion, nature or dreams. Symbols link the individual who often feels isolated and powerless, to that unites, something moving, inspiring and meaningful.

This pattern of our little, personal self, linking to something bigger, is the very heart of being an individualist. Our true story is the one that makes sense for us, integrating the world within with the world without. That we are creatures who can make sense of our lives, and tell that story to others, makes life beautiful. Our souls open to the astonishing sweetness of life. We are no longer closed buds, or unripe, bitter fruit. We are open, ripe and beautiful, nourishing ourselves and nourishing others who are open to receive the richness that we are.

70 Individualist Relationships
Genuineness

Relationships are a space that people create between themselves and live in. You know the joys of friendship, of love and of working successfully in groups in conformist relationships. Now you are ready to take relating a step further. No more are your relationships merely conditioned by social niceness, expectations and cooperation. A more subtle dance begins between you and others. It's the dance of being both cooperative and genuine!

Being genuine has two parts to it. First, you personally get clear about where you are on any given issue. Secondly, you share yourself as gently or as forcefully as the situation calls for.

After a lifetime of conformist conditioning, being clear about your feelings and thoughts is a whole new way of relating. You have to see through layers of repression that you have learned in order to fit in, first as a child and then as a cooperative and successful adult in the world. You begin to thaw the forbidden regions of your frozen self. How do you do that?

The good news is that a lot of growing happens naturally, with you developing more mature and flexible ways day by day. This natural process includes, as an individualist, your relating standards starting to go beyond the norm, as you feel stifled. Inwardly you may feel that you are suffocating, feeling unheard, restless, frustrated, angry or even depressed. Outwardly, you may be agreeable, while feeling phony, misunderstood, put down or not belonging. This can only last so long. Sooner or later something will slip out to voice what is going on with you. And it may not be pretty.

To make genuine relating more conscious, it's always good to sit alone and reflect on your own situation and get really familiar with your reactions to things. In your mind's eye, look at both sides, the other and you, and what triggers what. Reflecting on yourself, but in an accepting, nonjudgmental way, often begins to thaw your frozen self. You start to get insight into what's going on and why. Ways to enhance your loosening up also include talking to a trusted, receptive friend. This person doesn't fix you; he or she just listens and helps you understand. It is a great way to explore what you really feel and think. So is journaling, where you privately explore new edges to who you are. Books, classes, groups or professional support can be unimaginably helpful and transformative. Inner work and prayer may relate you powerfully to strengths within.

As you explore the denied, repressed and even forbidden in yourself, little by little it becomes less scary, less powerful to you. You can look, can see and can get insight into what was once simply not allowed. It doesn't mean that you have to act out or go crazy. You have the personal freedom to see, but not respond. We are all hard wired with a personal freedom center. When you sit alone and reflect on yourself, you strengthen your personal freedom center.

When the time comes to share yourself gently or forcefully, as the case may be, you are now more sure of yourself and can try out a more genuine level of relating. You can make use of tactful approaches to communicate. It is tactful to sandwich a "criticism" between positive statements. You might make "I" statements, not "you" statements. You are clear, saying things like, "When you do

...., I feel ...., and what I need is ...." In this way, you genuinely and clearly and usefully communicate. For example, When you get angry, I feel scared. I need you to control your anger.

Being honest, open and tactful is about respect, first for yourself, for the other and for your relationship. As an individualist, you are increasingly more conscious of feelings and complexities and your need for genuine expression. Co-dependency and enmeshment patterns may continue, but you can see them now and do something about them. You help yourself get free, and help the other get free, and so help in freeing up life everywhere.

Doing relationships in a genuine way creates clarity, trust and, paradoxically, increased closeness. If genuineness works, it's beautiful. If not, it may be genuine to move on.

71 Individualist Emotions
Recognizing and Expressing Emotions

Emotions, your instinctive feelings, passions and longings, rising up before you can think, are your personal advisors in moment-to-moment living. The good news is that keeping emotions in check in polite society serves you well in your social life. The bad news is that keeping your emotions in check shuts down your sensitivity to feelings in the name of getting along.

As an individualist, you value opening up your emotional awareness and it is a skill you are more and more comfortable with. Recognizing an emotion means, first of all, that you actually realize you are feeling something. We can be so shut down, that we don't know we are having an emotion.

I'm feeling something. What am I feeling? People make fun of therapists for asking, "How does that make you feel?" Yet naming what you feel is the pathway to waking up your personal self from the shutdown of everyday conformist society.

So when you get emotional, ask yourself, What am I feeling? Our emotions instinctively respond to others. Simply stated, we either feel safe or scared. So start with, I feel safe or unsafe. I feel good or bad. I feel attracted or turned off. Gradually you will name emotions with far greater richness. I feel happy, connected, affirmed, loving, joyful, recognized, appreciated, understood, respected or deeply loved. Or I feel sad, lonely, shame, anger, hatred, chagrin, dismay, ignored, "dissed" or hated.

Once you have named the emotion, you have done two important things. You have identified a feeling. And by naming it, secondly, you have gotten a distance on the feeling. Whenever you can "talk" about something, even in your own mind, such as, by naming a feeling, you have strengthened your personal freedom center. This naming creates the disconnect from the impulse to act out. This mindfulness means that you look before you leap, you think before you speak. It allows you to express emotions, even powerful ones, with a kind of detachment, in a simmered down version, not a boiling-hot explosion.

Getting good at recognizing and expressing emotions opens you to your inner richness of complexities and contradictions. Yes, they may tie you up in knots, but now you know what they are. This familiarity with inner contradictions and complexities may be confusing to the logical mind, but it is very familiar to our inner world. In fact, the world of psyche is complexity itself, and is most eager to be explored and untangled and known.

Active imagination can increase emotional awareness. In your mind's eye, you might attach an image to an emotion, like a person, a place or perhaps some words, maybe an association with your past. Gently receiving these inner messages amplifies your awareness, possibly creating an "aha" of insight. Soon you may discover an entire inner cast of characters, the good, the bad and the ugly. You might have these inner characters talk to each other. Pretty soon a lot of your contradictions are made conscious. Sometimes we resolve them and sometimes not. We consciously live with them. The resulting new, inner loosening up is remarkable.

Emotions affect your health. Anger is associated with heart disease. Feelings of helplessness seem connected to certain diseases such as diabetes or fibromyalgia. Love and strong social ties strengthen your health and increase longevity. So do faith and hope and doing good, selfless deeds. Spiritual practices reduce stress. Stress is related to poorer health in general. A sense of control improves health. So do optimism, strong self-love and a fighting spirit. Humor and laughter are healers.

Coming to recognize and name emotions, seeing the inner knots, loosening them, sitting with them in your personal freedom center, is a rich, and often funny experience. We begin to be awe struck at our inner cast of characters, all wanting power and showing it through emotions and passions. Our personal freedom center allows us to choose not to act on what we feel. This inner control, this richness of awareness, leads to increasing personal freedom and well-being, which is the ultimate goal of our emotional lives.

72 Individualist Ethics
Personal Integrity

Ethics, a code of right behavior that guides personal choices in self-control, self-awareness and social conscience, moves into a more subtle, personally responsible mode, as a person becomes an individualist. Individual dignity, with its core of personal freedom, becomes all-important. The emphasis is on the human spirit and its growth into personal integrity, rather than the outer control of authority, which worked so well in times past. Your right behavior in thought, word and deed is now more subtle and more self-directed. No outer authority could ever require the standards that your own integrity now demands of you from within.

This shift into a more personally responsible life begins by taking yourself more seriously. You follow the lead of your own soul, integrating within yourself, in a beautiful integral rhythm, a yin and yang of solitude and sociability, doing and being, thinking and feeling, rest and action, logic and dreams, body and soul.

So, what does personal integrity look like and what does it require of you? Integrity looks like a personal world that has come together on many levels. The little self of survival, doing and belonging and the big Self of authenticity and being are working together more and more. You can do your work and your relationships with skill and creativity. As dreams, yearnings and religious impulses make themselves known to you, you take their promptings seriously. They are the call of your deepest Self to live a more magnificent life, demanding a personal commitment to the highest and most demanding inspirations of the human spirit. How and where you participate in society is now more sharply focused. Your choices reflect and strengthen this more integral life that is now your path.

Your self-control now integrates your beliefs, your values and your behavior. The world within demands inner coherence. The world without must be lived from this inner coherence. The inner and the outer must match up, creating an integral sense of yourself within and yourself without. No longer are you a house divided against itself.

To achieve this astonishing maturity requires the deepest trust and receptivity for your personal experience, for your soul's innate wisdom, dignity, freedom and drive for self-actualization. Your deep experience of this world of soul is now becoming a familiar world to you. Its unexpected riches of beauty, truth and goodness are becoming the basis of what you think life is all about. Not only for you, but it becomes the basis of how to treat everyone. No longer can you look out onto the world with double standards. It is impossible to have such a deeply rich personal life, without a similar respect for it in others as well. What is good is what affirms personal freedom and dignity, not only yours but everyone's. What is bad is what takes personal freedom and dignity away, anywhere.

As you hold yourself to a higher standard, you wonder how to relate to others who need your guidance, such as students or children. Or, how you ought to react when you see others making needy, non-aware, savvy, sassy, or not too reflective decisions. How do you live in a world in which you disagree with others' ethics? How can you live in a world where you now see that people all around you are in different places in the spiral of life?

Often you judge what you see as evil. Are you to hold others to the same demanding standards by which you live?

The wisest ones suggest that it is best to observe all and act on little. You believe that we are all interconnected and somehow that other person is you, participating in the same universal life forces as you. So within yourself you know the very qualities that are in the other. When you act, you do so with tact and compassion and love, remembering that everyone has their rightful place in the spiral of life. You realize that your integration is a microcosm of the world's, and maybe, as with "the butterfly effect," it even provides a nudge in the whole world's liberation from chaos.

73 Individualist Awareness
Soul

Awareness as an individualist takes a gigantic leap from conformist doing and being. Individualist awareness opens up the eye of soul. You are at a deeper place within yourself, one less affected by day-to-day demands and conditioning. You open the eye of soul not by a familiar determination to be in charge and make things happen. It is actually quite the opposite.

You open your eye of soul (also known as the mind's eye) by letting worlds come to you, and letting them affect you. In other words you become receptive. You allow yourself to receive impressions, get information, to become impassioned, to be transported, to experience awe.

You know these many worlds through the many ways of knowing, be it body language, the running thoughts and images of your mind, and your relationships in the world. Some are personal. Others are more universal in nature and may be spoken of as "collective." And to some of these many impressions, you may experience a strong personal response, if you have open the eye of soul.

In the world of body, the eye of soul receives body symptoms or its spontaneous movement for "body talk" messages. It uses active imagination to amplify messages so that you can "get it." In the world of mind, the mind's eye reflects on both the mind's content and on its process. It considers its images and spontaneous thoughts, as well as the endless rising and falling of the mind's stream of consciousness. Finally, in your relationship to the world, the inner eye reflects on what attracts and what repels. It attempts to see honestly. It tries to integrate such daily life signals in into your personal direction and, perhaps, even into a philosophy of life.

As an example, the mind's eye might receive impressions from the body. It observes how the body feels or spontaneously. There can be a simple scanning from head to toe for areas of comfort or discomfort. Realms of comfort may be expanded in your mind's eye to extend them wherever you wish. Your body comfort zones may actually follow the lead of your mind's eye, but not always. Practice helps.

You can also focus on realms of discomfort with active imagination to amplify the body symptom. You allow the symptom to take on color, shape or even an imagined person, in your mind's eye. This imaginal presence can have a voice, or may need to act out something, or may need to change into something else. This acting out may even inspire you to allow spontaneous movements of your body to take place, in order to get more insight.

If you get an "aha," that is, a message, through this active imagination, you might take it one step further. Do so by asking yourself this most essential question: What does this new awareness remind me of in my daily life now? In such a way body innerwork may tell you what needs to happen next in your life. Interestingly, it is very common for body discomfort to go away through this innerwork. It may go away because you finally got the message!

Ancients spoke of the soul loving beauty, truth and goodness. We may experience these in loving a sunset or being moved by music. Or we may get the message of an insightful movie or a good book. Family, friends and or a lover may enchant us with the goodness of their love.

183

From the collective realm, the possibilities of being moved are infinite. Rituals, symbols and even propaganda can powerfully stir your soul. So, be careful of the God, the gods or the causes that you let in. Aphrodite inspires you to be the enchanting lover. Self-righteous causes may inspire hate and destruction. Parenthood may lead to domestic tranquility and selfless patience with your children. A God of love may lead you to become a saint.

The realm of soul opens a vastly larger world than conformist life affords. In the soul's freedom and fluidity you may sense that you seem to understand more of the realm of Spirit itself. Spirit is continuously rising and falling, shape-shifting in time, through the myriad layers of human development and awareness, as mist shifts shape over a summer morning lake. When you open your mind's eye, you both observe Spirit's infinite freedom and fluidity everywhere, and also see it manifesting in yourself. Reality becomes multilayered, with the personal and the universal making a coherent whole, when seen with the eye of soul.

74 Individualist Wisdom
Inner Meaning

We live in our private worlds and comfort zones of illusion. Much of it is conditioned by the culture we live in. Much of our comfort zone comes from how we want things to be. We hold on to the idea that all is going well: life is good; things are going to be OK; we act as though we will live forever! So we try to keep our world intact, even as it is disappearing right before our eyes, our youth, the people we love, good times, pretty things and even hard won success. When the bubble breaks, and the conventional answers to suffering and loss don't work anymore, we are forced to either ignore our pain or look further.

Looking further to find personal meaning starts you thinking, behaving and relating in a more honest and thoughtful way. You are much more of an acute observer than you had been. This mindfulness, this receptive awareness of things around you and within you, is liberating for you. Being an observer without being pulled in, without judgment, makes you feel free inside, giving you insight into others and greater personal security and flexibility for yourself. You even begin to value mindfulness itself for its enriching and liberating effects.

This experience of inner freedom becomes the gateway to look further into your inner life. You see the workings of the soul within you, finding a world very different from everyday life. It is more inclusive and seemingly wiser than our everyday self. The strength of the inner world may both startle you with its nearness, and thrill you with its richness and empowerment and satisfaction.

The inner world reveals itself to you in simple, creative and symbolic ways, as you turn inward. Receptive mindfulness opens you powerfully to meaning within. You use solitude, simple sitting, meditation, perhaps art and much quiet to find your own inner truth. Perhaps other spiritual practices work for you, as well, such as those of spiritual reading, of ritual, of sacraments, prayer, fasting and compassionate good works.

Or you may use any one of alternative innerwork practices to go within. These innerwork practices can include connecting to holy figures in a given tradition or connecting to a wise personal guide within you. You might use active imagination, stream of consciousness, go on spirit journeys as do shamans, or honor meaningful coincidences in your daily life. Altered states of consciousness may expand your knowing.

Out of this receptive way of seeing, entire new worlds of meaning and being in the world open up for you. You start getting insights, feeling inspiration and "aha's" in your gut. You are surprised how these seemingly insignificant soul messages give guidance, satisfy, empower and give you peace. And most importantly, you work to integrate your newfound meaning into your conscious, daily life of doing and belonging in the larger world.

Artistic, educational, psychological and religious groups all set standards for the right ways and the wrong ways of doing the inner life. Each tradition has its interpretation of what is true and good and beautiful in doing the inner life. And they profoundly contradict each other. These opinions often focus on the founder, the founding values, visions, traditions and the practices that follow. Very few traditions integrate the many ways of knowing into a cohesive whole, as does Lifewheel.

The paths are myriad. They vary dramatically in insight, freedom and compassion. Yet note that all of these growth traditions have one thing in common. They all value the unseen, inner world and seek to intensify its reality. The inner life is seen as real, perhaps more real and in some ways more reliable than mundane, changeable, everyday life.

Humans cannot live without meaning. And so we are artists, storytellers, mythmakers, philosophers, dreamers and worshippers. Your meaning may be that there is no meaning and you find meaning in that. Then that is your story, your myth. That interpretation, however, may close the door to further gifts of the inner world. The inner world can connect with a limitless world of empowerment, inspiration, enchantment, freedom and freshness. It enlivens you and your life story and gives meaning to your life. Your very soul may depend on seeing with the mind's eye, your eye of soul.

Kathy Kouzmanoff

Individualist Social Development

75 Individualist Family
Family Of Origin, Committed Relationships and Support Circles

It may come as a surprise to conventional family types that there are many, varied and contradictory ways to be family. Family is a group of people sharing a common origin, a common vision, commitment or supportive lifestyle.   Much social change is eventually considered acceptable, but often it starts out in seemingly oddball groups, as seen from the eye of the conformist. Individuals who move out of the conventional patterns may look for new support circles.   There distinctiveness finds kinship, as individuals are understood and promoted.

So what do these more individualist families look like?   They usually share something that sets them apart from the conventional ways.   The family of origin norm of a married man and woman, with children and close intergenerational ties is the conventional norm.   Mom is homemaker and dad is out working to support the family.   It's obvious how traditional such a pattern is.

Individualist family variations on that norm are everywhere. Women work outside the home.   Men stay home and are househusbands. Couples don't have children. Kids of another race are adopted.   Grandparents raise kids.   A man and a woman live together without marriage.   There are sexless marriages and companionship marriages.   There are even marriages devoted to important work or the arts or love of God.   Couples divorce and marry others, sometimes several times in a lifetime.   Same sex couples set up households, having children. They seek legal marriage status, with the full legal rights of spouses.

There are celibate religious families, intentional communities, ashrams, cooperatives, universities and artist colonies. AA and their Twelve Step groups, retirement communities, expatriate groups, military families, corporate career families and government service groups. They are all oriented around a common need that is more specifically focused than conventional life. The groups strengthen identity and provide vital social support.

Conventional types may judge some of these groups as unattractive, strange or eccentric, deeply self-indulgent, weird or even evil. But a deep social need for these kinship groups exists for individualists. The individualist has outgrown, or perhaps never fully identified with, the norm.

Individualist marriages value their partner's self-expression and self-actualization. They encourage individual freedom, rather than conformity. This is extended to the children as well. This is not a license to be selfish. Rather, it is a challenge to foster self-development within commitment. It values freedom within family support. Being different is honored for the special gifts it brings. Children are taught responsible expression of their individual freedom. Problems are worked through and not repressed. Your family is a place to ask for help when necessary. It is OK to ask and OK to help. Painful conflicts between love and work may arise. They may lead to painful compromises or change. They are faced thoughtfully and honestly and respectfully.

Your family of origin gives you a distinctive personality heritage. Its history, values and genetic codes shape you powerfully. You realize their influences. And you have made peace with them. You do this as you differentiate into your own individual self.

Individualist family groups attempt to provide stability and encourage growth in their members. Honesty with respect is the norm. Riding the edge of ongoing development is exciting Individualist families do the dance of mutual support and personal individuality.

76 Individualist Politics
Personal Rights, Public Good, Public Safety and Public Office

Imagine a political system based on integrity. Politicians support equal opportunity in education and economics and the protection of the law. They vote for the common good. They avoid personal gain and special interests, also the cynical and hateful. Imagine a political system with checks and balances. Imagine the constant renewal of leaders.

If this sounds a lot like the government of the United States as it was envisioned when it was founded, you would be right. In fact, these high individualist standards of government are the conformist norm in American government. Politicians give lip service to them all the time. Any true democracy would reflect these values. Any country that has these founding principles can be very proud, indeed, of their place in the spiral of life.

The idealism of this level of governing is inspiring, yet is easily soured by hard realities of how democratic power often plays out. There are special interests, corrupt use of power, greed and incompetence. So, how does one overcome these difficulties and do individualist politics?

The name of the game is compromise, giving a little to get a little. Idealists are often impatient with such reality politics. Yet realistic idealists think big and act small. They think global and act local. A little step in the right direction is the way to go.

Respectful politics is not hate politics. It does not use emotional smear tactics in confronting those of differing opinions. Respectful politics uses the high art of diplomacy. It is looking for where we can agree. Always the aim is of peaceful coexistence through justice for all and resolution of differences. A lot of politics these days is a long way from this level of civility.

A politician represents the interests of his or her constituency, and also has to stay true to his or her personal political philosophy as well. You believe you serve them best by keeping to your ideals for which you were elected.

Because the individual is of highest value, individualist politics seek to ensure individual liberties over the power interests of government. Personal freedom is what democracy is all about, and if we err, we err on the side of individual freedom.

Likewise, the individual pursuit of happiness, as supported in the American Declaration of Independence, is a value highly prized and is of utmost priority. This value is not one of license, taking things back to a naïve and narcissistic level. An individualist pursuit of happiness respects the right to pursue happiness for each individual. Individual rights are balanced by the common good. The right to bear arms is balanced by utmost caution in their use. Justice for crimes committed is balanced by gentle mercy.

Personal rights encourage self-development, but need the active support of educational and economic opportunity for all. The very success of a democracy may forget that those rising up need opportunity the most.

Volunteering in a political campaign finds you doing hard work, realistic work, because you understand that this is the practical way to deal with the realities of a true democracy. Politics is a tough arena and you are willing to deal with its hard realities, inspired by universal ideals. No government is ever going to create a perfect world. You maintain your commitment to your ideals through ongoing personal renewal, especially from a place deep within yourself.

Democratic ideals stir the human heart to participate in the public forum. The original ideals of universal brotherhood are the only thing strong enough to overcome our disgust with misdirected policies, injustice and misuse of power. If your heart is stirred with passion for the true ideals of democracy, you are most needed in the public arena. Crippling cynicism may be a reflection of your own compromises and powerlessness. Get thee renewed. True democracy is an ideal that can inspire ever greater universal justice and freedom, and selfless service on their behalf.

77 Individualist Religion/Arts
Art, Philosophy, Psychology and Religion

Individualists put the highest value on traditions promoting religious and aesthetic freedom. Absolute freedom, of inquiry and expression, for each individual soul, is the ultimate value for an individualist. Universities, private institutes and religious traditions can be found with rich traditions to support this freedom. There are innumerable schools of art, religious traditions, writings of philosophers and thinkers in transpersonal psychology for you to consider. Through such seemingly endless riches, you too may see that, in a manner of speaking, God has a thousand faces.

So, if there are so many varied expressions of the ultimate, why bother trying to figure it out at all? What is the point?

The point is you! Your reflections have taken you to this point on your journey. Now some inner urgency pushes you on to have your own personally refined, and more subtle, knowing of ultimacy. You seek your own meaningful link to something timeless. You realize that this is now an intensely personal journey. You measure success by your own internal standards of knowing that you have arrived. Your personal salvation now consists of finding your own beauty, truth and goodness, and giving it meaningful expression in the world.

Whatever your personality type is, it finds its most mature expression in the religious style most suitable to you, and not someone else's. The introverted, thinking type may look to a unified way of understanding the nature of things. The idealist may seek a harmony that unifies many facets of reality into a cohesive whole. The extravert may look to selfless, good works, or devotional spiritual practices that really do renew one's spirit. Your spiritual striving now knows the style or styles best for your personality. To do spiritual seeking in a style not yours, naturally, would feel confusing, discordant and perhaps meaningless.

In your own art work, self-exploration and self-expression through your art are the goals. In other's art, you go for the unique, the unusual and the highly personal. You put high value on distinctive forms of expression. You look for someone's work that you resonate with. You also look for art that moves your soul, perhaps, to the point of awe.

Religious institutions provide a place for you to develop your capacity for reflection and insight. An institution's practical experience and rich traditions may serve your growth well. Your purpose in joining an art school a personal growth group or a religious institution is to reflect on their experience and rich traditions, in a deep and personally meaningful way. You no longer look for someone to simply give you the "right" answers. You might also look for a fellowship of kindred spirits, in social institutions that synergize your beliefs and values.

Your personal life experience causes you to reflect deeply and perhaps to reach out to others for additional learning and kinship. You take in what fits and reject what doesn't. You most value religious institutions or personal growth groups for their support, as you reflect and deal with reality thoughtfully. You value traditions that have gone ahead of you, as you mindfully give them consideration. You may find that eventually you make your own unique contribution to the ongoing development of human spirit in time.

78 Individualist Sex/Closeness
Eroticism, Sex, Connectedness, Love, Communication,
Masculine and Feminine Orientation

For the individualist, the double standards and lack of awareness in conformist sex and closeness are transformed. Closeness is more aware, more honest and often experienced as a rich, freely chosen freedom in commitment.

Love is born of the eyes and heart, a medieval poem exclaims. This romantic love is a deeply personal response to the sight of the beloved. It is a powerfully erotic force, highly charged, and deeply binding lovers to each other. It is not a love arranged by family, politics or church traditions. Romantic love may even break the codes of social appropriateness. Natural attraction is the basis of non-exclusive friendships as well, and the affectionate bond may also be palpably strong.

Personal needs, projections and illusions are often a part of romantic love and natural attraction. The individualist enters into such attractions with far greater self-awareness and self-understanding. You probably realize why this particular person has romantically smote you, or why you so enjoy a particular new friend. Part of your self-awareness may be realizing the power of inspiration to energize you. You may consciously choose an archetype, such as Aphrodite or a heroic lover, to energize your part in a relationship.

This deepened self-awareness also allows your sexual relating greater freedom, honesty and complexity. You have more realistic expectations of the consequences of your involvement. You may choose a relationship for lust or love. But you are aware of the difference and are honest about it with your partner. Your decisions responsibly take other relationships and commitments into account. You are less naïve than you were about the negative impact of relating to someone of questionable character. You know the cost to your personal karma of relating casually or relating simply for your own personal gain.

Your connections may be highly individualized. Maybe you were childhood sweethearts or share a special interest. You may have a biracial or gay relationship. Maybe it's an older woman/younger man pattern or older man/younger woman that attracts. Some people want to have their individuality mirrored. Others love the challenge that opposites attract, and they can live with the tension. The erotic even includes the normal effects of aging, suffering or sickness on your lover or friend. In fact, you may find others more endearing as you watch them changing with time. After all, you're changing too!

Your conversations are increasingly more sensitive to the other and more nuanced. Your own deepening self gives you the strength to be close to others, with both genuine warmth and cautious candor. Your increased personal freedom allows you to be socially accommodating when needed, or to go for more depth and candor, when that seems appropriate. Your freedom of expression often leads to richness and delight in others.

Sexual imagery expands its meaning for the individualist. It no longer merely means simple lust or conventional physical attraction. The individualist may consciously choose highly personalized sexual behavior for self-expression, while often keeping it hidden from conventional society. Sexual imagery in dreams may be seen as a metaphor for connection or closeness to another person, or to what they stand for. In Hindu religious temples, a couple in sexual embrace may be at the temple entrance. This embrace represents the bliss of the human soul in intimate embrace with the divine.

The erotic creates a feeling of connection or oneness with the beloved. In a way, you submit to being taken over by love. If you do this consciously, the pattern of receptivity is strengthened, a pattern that is so much a part of impassioned, expanded, soulful living.

79 Individualist Social Situations
Food, Shelter, Clothing, Cyberspace, Society and Time

You no longer identify with conformist ways of doing things, even though you probably share much with how most people do things in your culture. As an individualist, at least part of your social life expresses your individualist side. Your decisions may be made with awareness of how they affect others and how they impact the planet. These options require a strong commitment to the cause of sustainability. Until it becomes more the norm, it is still difficult to live green in mass culture. For many individualists, who pour their lives into their special causes, interests or self-development, their surroundings and food may remain quite ordinary.

Social life is dramatically impacted by economics. Your capacity for self-expression in food, shelter and clothing, cyberspace, society and time may be a luxury of the privileged affluent in an industrialized country. Self-expression in society may not even be an option for most in entire cultures.

Food, shelter and clothing may become more a matter of conscious choice, when considering sustainability and future generations. There may be buying local, organic, eating vegetarian, composting, raising your own food and supporting sustainable agriculture. Eating a healthy diet of high fiber, moderate protein and carbohydrates, with healthy fats, is often a standard way of eating in less developed countries, but requires informed choices in wealthy cultures.

Home styles may or may not reflect your individualist values. If your home does reflect you as an individualist, it could express what you love, your history and probably your personality. Traditionalists would show the continuity of generations with heirlooms and photos and icons of religious tradition or education. Experiencers would have a home with travel mementos and ongoing projects with food, plants, hobbies and games. Conceptualizers' love of books would be obvious by their libraries and their tinkering. Idealists might fully coordinate the décor, and as an individualist, it would be a coordination that inspires them, with its beauty and personal significance.

Again dress is highly individualistic and often deceiving. Extraverts probably pay more attention to how they dress than introverts. The casual look of the preoccupied professor comes to mind. Socially conscious dressers may recycle, shop resale and buy less than they can afford. They may also try to buy local and green, avoid sweatshop made products and stores that exploit employees. When self-expression does take place through clothing, the style is often one's own, and not entirely following current fashions. What one values, be it native cultures, beauty, quality, or the need to make an artistic statement, could all come through dress.

Your use of time is as much as possible under your control, in order to meet your own objectives. You deeply value freedom from daily routines, so you can do your thing. You are also aware that there are many facets and attitudes to time. Things take time. Time marches on, and time waits for no one. Time has cycles and seasons. Sometimes time seems to fly by, and other times it seems to drag. There is clock time and dreamtime. There is work time and beach time.

Cars, household goods, vacations, modes of travel, use of cyberspace, all probably reflect an amazing combination of conformity and individualist style, perhaps even some responder and conscient choices as well. You especially prize interesting new faces and exotic new places. You find animals interesting, in their own way, and treat them with responsibility and respect. You use money, drugs and alcohol with responsibility for your own reasons.

You share your resources with others, as the situation allows. Your social life is for your own reasons, and it matters little if you see or are seen in the "right places." You join groups to grow and learn and express your identity. You seek out neighborhoods, people and organizations that support and reflect your individuality and values. You see universal health care supporting the poor and the old, the valuable self-employed, who often are the cutting edge, risk taking and creative members of society.

80 Individualist Work
Money, Livelihood, Hobbies, Special Interests, Daily Routines, Useful Activity

Working not just for money, but because it is personally meaningful to you, takes center stage as an individualist. The challenge may be more demanding, but it is also more self-expressive, self-actualizing and more fulfilling. The inspiration comes from within; the commitment does too. The work itself becomes the motivation, not the paycheck, not the toys you can buy. Bringing inspiration into concrete manifestation is soulful work, be it in a new discovery, cure, invention, piece of art, healed relationship or greater inner well-being.

Usually what creates meaning in life is a link between you and your genuine expression in the outer world. Extraverts find the cause that inspires. Introverts find the self-expression that satisfies. Both seek connection between something meaningful within and something meaningful without, just finding a different energizing point.

Meaningful work can be on yourself, for yourself. Therapy may release you from unconscious trauma. Analysis may open the world of the transpersonal to you through dreams, inner symbols and altered states. Spiritual conversion may link you through teachings, traditions and practices to a faithful presence beyond yourself within yourself. All this innerwork creates relationships to others as coaches, analysts, teachers, mentors, friends, as well as in the brotherhood and sisterhood of fellow believers.

Self-healing and self-discovery are powerful, generating a motivation to shout it from the rooftops, hoping to share new worlds within with others. Your personal issues or difficulties that have led to your healing, create a wounded healer, one who has suffered and recovered and brings compassion to others who are wounded. You need not be perfect to make a difference. Great inspiration comes to the wounded ones as they heal. Great contributions to others can come from these wounded ones.

You have become a reliable, honest and straightforward person, mixing truth with tact. You no longer simply conform in order to get along. Your increasing self-awareness and self-expression give you deepened respect for others' equal importance to you. Your personal integrity respects the dignity of others, as you try not to dump your frustrations on them.

You desire right work, which provides self-expression and self-actualization. You have skills and knowledge that challenge you almost beyond reach, yet continue to fascinate and beckon. Work, where you continue to follow the lead of your inspiration and the commitment, is riveting. The work is its own reward. Personal expression and accomplishment come together. Meaningful work may be in any area, raising kids, the sciences, the social services, farming, journalism, the military or politics. It is wherever you find inspiration that leads to commitment, self-sacrifice for the greater good and deep personal fulfillment.

You offer the workplace and the public your best in value driven service. Working for others is done with the spirit of service, inspiration, healing, fun, humor and beauty. You care, continuously renewed by an inner source that keeps you fresh, hopeful, lively, healed and renewed.

If there is no personal internal connection to your work, there is no meaning. Cynicism or despair set in. Meaning requires that we live by the demands of our stage in life. As a child we play and grow and learn. As a young adult we find our way to where we belong, in love and work. As a midlife adult we do the work of soul, linking ourselves to something personally meaningful. As a fully mature, ripe adult, we revel in our richness, finding life lush, mysterious and joyous. So meaning reflects the work of our own developmental stages. It all has its place in the spiral of life.

Level 4   Conscient

Conscient Basics

Conscious and Connected

Spirit

(Enlightened Ego in Service of Self/No Ego)

Basic Task: To Be Aware Of The Subtlety And Interconnectedness Of All Things
Basic Value: Being
Basic Belief: All Is As It Is.
Basic Problem: No Problem
Motto: *Sometimes I Sits and Thinks and Sometimes I Just Sits.* OR *Love One Another*

81 Conscient Description
Conscious and Connected (Spirit)

The experiences of a lifetime have softened your heart and opened you. You are more understanding and more inclusive. Yet, despite all the changes you have experienced in your life, you are unchanged at the core, still the same. You belong to two realities, one fleeting and one constant. You no longer identify with just the fleeting. You identify more and more with the unchanging being that you are. This conscient living often happens after age fifty, although you may experience breakthroughs at any time of your life.

From this dual perspective, you are able to live with paradox. Contradictions abound, but they are only apparent. You develop, yet you are always the same. You sometimes regress backwards, yet you still feel free, beyond limits of your own neediness, doing, belonging, or personal self-actualization.

You live with mindfulness, that gentle openness, where there are both freedom and stability, awareness and letting be, complexity and simplicity, justice and compassion, hope and acceptance, helping hands and simple being.

You do regular innerwork practices, including just sitting quietly, continually re-anchoring your deep knowing and interconnected being. You live in deep awareness of the present, experiencing timelessness in time, having a spontaneous joy and universal loving flow. You observe all as it is, and mostly know that it is so, and let it be. You live in keeping with natural rhythms within yourself and the planet. Your work and relationships are rich and harmonious.

Which growth tradition you believe in matters less than the freedom place to which they all lead. You express this awareness to others in the joy of simply being together. Simplicity in all things outward is more and more your style, as your inner life gains in increasingly interconnecting richness.

Your sexuality and communication reflect timeless qualities of genuine spontaneity, delight, union and joy. You want less to be known than to know, less to receive than to give, less to be understood than to understand, less to be loved than to love.

The wisdom you possess and the love that moves you, allow you to overcome despair. You have achieved an intimate union with Being itself, a kind of oneness that puts an end to all of your yearnings and seeking.

Your sense of humor is rich, allowing you to see the limits of human foibles and the utter seriousness with which we take them. This even includes humor in the all too serious intellectual pursuits and ceremony of religions. The conscient eye is free to see that they are but a means and an arrow pointing the way, not the end in itself.

The shadow side of conscient being shows itself in many ways, though, too. You can develop a grossly inflated sense of your own importance and abandon a personal common touch. Or you can cease to respect the boundaries and taboos, which protect others' dignity. You might become impatient with those who have not yet arrived at your seemingly high level, not giving others their own rightful place and time in the spiral of life. You can also abandon common sense, and give yourself over to a guru or to spiritual teachings, which may be unsound, or do not respect boundaries and protective taboos.

You might also experience a "dark night of the soul," a feeling of inner aridity and even emptiness. Strange body sensations may sometimes arise. In Hinduism these are referred to as Kundalini energies, arising as your innerwork reduces energy blockages and awakens "sleeping energies" at the base of the spine. Finally, there is a fine line between enlightenment and madness, so a mental breakdown can occur, if you should become overwhelmed.

Responders may identify with your seeming simplicity, confusing it with non-awareness. Conformists may see you as baffling, or just plain stupid, from their smart, savvy and worldly perspective. Individualists often mistrust spiritual awakening as abandoning reasonable, hard-won consciousness.

The conscient stage can heal many wounds. Responders find healing for their neediness. Conformists seek peace lost from too much doing and belonging. Individualists catch a glimpse of total liberation from their efforts at personal self-actualizing or manifesting the timeless in time.

Conscients show a conscious and connected face when they are assessed in relation to common personality traits or preferences. Personality preferences between opposites, as listed below, (the preferences in a widely used personality indicator[18]), can all have a conscient level of development, as suggested here.

- The conscient *introvert* lives the paradox of inner, liberating bliss and outward, heartfelt connectedness. The *extravert* experiences both committed love and inner freedom.

- The *sensing* type mindfully observes details, often from many perspectives or ways of knowing. The *intuitive type* experiences spontaneous insight into how things are.

- The *thinking type* uses paradox as the highest form of logic, where time and timelessness are both true at once. The *feeling type* lets the continuous stream of emotion rise and fall, observing and letting it move on.

- The *ordering type (or judger)* and the *go with the flow type* (or *perceiver)* find balance in each other. Focus and flow come together, making daily life seem effortless, as life is lived in focused flow, slow, orderly and entrained.

Some basic personality traits that are often viewed as indicators of a healthy personality can show conscient level development.

Emotional stability is stable, open and free. Your emotions flow freely, yet your inner freedom lets you observe them all, choosing what to act on, respectfully share or simply let be.

Agreeableness is outwardly harmonious and inwardly congruent. There is no other and no enemy, only the one ground of being, in which we meet, in openness and love.

Openness to new experience is free-flowing, observing the unbounded, free, rich flow of being in time. You not only observe all. You realize your kinship with all. Your participation is both dynamic and contained.

82 Conscient Basic Task
*To Be Aware of the Subtlety and Interconnectedness of
All Things*

Your basic task as a conscient is to step into another world that no one owns, but which is home to us all. It is everywhere. It is vast, sensitive, subtle and intelligent. Here the smallest of details are charged with vitality and connected with everything else.

Your entry into this world is everywhere. It's right here, right now, and it has the smallest of openings. It is this very moment rising up and falling away, as fresh as dew, as intense as a lover, as passing as your last breath. Your own mindful self enters the smallest of openings. As you sit in the realization of your own experience flowing moment to moment, you may break open into a blissful richness that is inexpressible, beyond details. You experience, as William Blake said, "eternity in a grain of sand."

When you enter this enchanted state of being, you may find it familiar. It is the feeling you get when you are on vacation. Or when you are in love. Or when you pray. It carries the awe of a sunset. Your own experience of the ordinary is charged with extraordinary vitality. The past and the future slip away. Everything is just this keen present interconnected now. You are more present, more aware, more connected and more alive.

83 Conscient Basic Value
Being

As a conscient, you live in a realm of richness not made by money. Here is the birthright of your original joy, a realm of peace, where there is enjoyment and, sometimes, even bliss in simple being. All are welcomed. Here is the place where it's possible for everyone to be in love with everyone else.

In being, you transcend common daily concerns with qualities of just being in the now, by just hanging out and simply being together. Simplicity and effortless, focused flow are a lifestyle. Often calm, serenity and simple being prevail. Playfulness, spontaneity, wild abandon and joyous noise are the fun side of losing your all too important little self.

At times, at the sudden appearance of utter destruction, grief may tear you open. You wail out the agony. Being is a house with two levels, one to the stream of time, with its hard-core street life. The other level to your house of being is free of suffering. Here is a home that can deal with it all.

With such qualities in place, you are poised to live with the keen immediacy of being. The present moment is all that is needed for your being house in time, where all is as it is. In this house you have nowhere to go, nothing to have, do or be. You already have everything. You already are everything. You know you were created for this state of grace. Open, balanced, entrained, you are the living joy, awe and love of your original self.

84 Conscient Basic Belief
All Is As It Is.

Life goes on, pretty much the same as it has before you, and so it will continue, after you as well. Things don't change much. Human nature is still going to be human nature, with its complexities in the spiral of life. Everyone is different and relationships are difficult. Social organization is full of imbalances, striving, injustice and failures.

Things are as they are. All is as it is.

Jesus said, "You will always have the poor with you." He also said, "Give unto Caesar the things that are Caesar's, and unto God the things that are God's." Hardly the words of a social activist, although he was known to clear the moneychangers out of the temple, in a fit of disgust!

Does this "realistic" acceptance of things as they are mean that you give up, that you are defeated, that one person ought not to try to make a difference? I don't think so. Things are as they are; you know that. And you still rage against the darkness, not going quietly. You are a living paradox. You find your perfection in the world of being, and you bring its inspiration into the world of time. You are a conscient, a bridge between two worlds.

85 Conscient Basic Problem
No Problem

Being conscient has brought you to a place of freedom, free of the opposites of time and timelessness. You understand how things are. Yet, in spite of the problems, you still care. You remain connected. You are coming into the world from your personal freedom place, where there is no problem.

You live with deep centeredness. You look out on the world, loving it and caring for it. You have found the way to both care about suffering and the limitations in life and to be free of them.

You are a bit like Kokopelli, the humorous, sometimes bawdy trickster god of the Native American Southwest. Or like S Elf, the Lifewheel mascot. Both see the uptight ways of humans and with a little mischief and sweetness, help to free imprisoned souls.

As a conscient, you very much have this attitude toward life. You have gained a distance, a perspective on things. You see things as they are. The urgency to do more, have more and be more is tempered. You simply are as you are, even as life unfolds all around. All is as it is. From your inner freedom place, there is no problem.

86 Conscient Motto
Sometimes I Sits and Thinks and Sometimes I Just Sits.
Love One Another

Sometimes I Sits and Thinks and Sometimes I Just Sits.

Just sitting. Not thinking about anything in particular. You know the feeling, that of a weekend morning, a day off, just hanging out with your kids. And then out of nowhere, that sudden breakout of joy! Or it can be on a bracing hiking trip or on the comforting back porch, or going for a beautiful drive, or having leisurely coffee, or passing a dramatic cityscape, or flying through sunlit clouds. Maybe it comes to you at organ music in a soaring cathedral, at a slow moving river, smooth and swirling all at once, or at dappled shadows on a fence's repeating pattern. Joy catches you unawares.

Love One Another

Love everyone, unconditionally, friend and enemy, without need, without requirement. How can one love so completely, so selflessly? There has to be a source for such loving. It isn't in our world of separateness, differences and constant change, with its rising up and falling away of all that we love and attempt to hold onto. This love comes from somewhere else, a place where I am you and you are me, where loving me is loving you, and loving you is loving me, and the loving is all that really matters.

Kathy Kouzmanoff

Conscient Personal Development

87 Conscient Motivation
Beyond Your Personal Self

There is only one aim now, to live the conscient life. Your mind and heart and personal fulfillment now live in a realm beyond your personal self. Your desire is to live without desire. Your aim in time is to live in the timeless present. You aim to be both mindful and mindless, focused and flowing, free and interconnected. Living from this realm of effortless activity, of creative quiet, manifests your timelessness in time.

The conscient life requires everything of you. You submit to the flow of things, to the Tao, to the big picture. Each choice you make is less about you, and more about right rhythm and the interconnection of all things. Nothing is denied. Nothing is alien. All is seen for what it is. Your choices serve this larger interconnection. You submission to this path, of how things are, makes you the selfless servant of life itself. Your little, personal, limited self-interest is long gone, dissolved into the greater whole.

Love is enchantment. Keen interest in others is immediate. Kinship and the open heart prevail. Sweet relating to others holds up to them a mirror of themselves. In seeing your glowing face, they remember their own radiant joy.

Such selflessness requires of you your utmost inner freedom and openness. Your openness to everyone and everything is alert and receptive. You observe, without desire or need or conditioning, simply allowing the moment to unfold. You see all and judge little. Your observing leans toward compassion. You choose this freedom place within again and again. Practicing it regularly keeps you centered and present and feeling acutely alive.

Even in times of inner dryness, you maintain regular practices to strengthen your inner self, knowing from experience, that your freedom and joy will return. Your banishment keeps you striving for a return to joy, where once again life is fresh, and you are mindful, loving, balanced, free and enchanted.

Your practices may include just sitting. Effortlessly you are renewed by silence or nature or beauty. You reflect on how things are, perhaps by journaling, reading or praying. Other times you may participate in spiritual rituals. You might return to your deeper self through the repetitive rhythms in drumming, music or those of your own breath. You find support in your growth community of fellow seekers. Sacred places inspire.

Intention is a gateway for you. What you intend is clear, and you put it forth with confidence. You live with the deep expectancy that what you intend will come to be. Intention opens hidden doors. The road unfolds ahead of you, not always as you expected, but leading in the direction of your deepest, intended desire. Such unfolding is witness of your connection to a larger, conscious, subtle and powerful reality.

You mostly live in the moment. The present moment contains everything that you need. In the present, if you have openness enough and emptiness enough, you may find infinite richness. You return to the present again and again. There is nothing but this eternal, boundless, unlimited now.

Even your humor is keenly insightful, subtle and sweet. It may be at the expense of spiritual beliefs and of you, sometimes aiming to teach, but never to demean. Often conscient humor juxtaposes time and timelessness for humans from hilarious new angles, as in the jokes of questionable arrivals at the Pearly Gates.

Everything is the richness of Spirit endlessly manifesting in time. Everything is metaphor for Spirit. Everything is but one taste, the taste of Spirit. The destination and the journey merge. You desire nothing. You are part of Spirit's great enlivening, manifesting in time. Your personal self nests in this great web of unfolding. This is the fulfillment of all your striving, to know that all you have been, and all you may yet be, are part of Spirit's great unfolding, now and now and now.

88 Conscient Identity
Transpersonal

You have come a long way on the journey of life. Once you were mostly needy, naïve, narcissistic and non-aware. You learned to be smart, savvy, sassy and successful in the world. And you awakened, more and more, by being reflective, receptive and real, to how things really are, in yourself and in the world. Yet all the changes haven't taken the real you away. Your body is aging, yet you feel young and fresh. The real you is still there, but more fluid, more aware and more kind.

No matter where you are in the spiral of life, you sense the presence of this truer, deeper, more mindful self. You know it well. You are strong yet fluid and open. You are inwardly centered, yet outwardly connected. You are grounded yet flexible, complex yet coherent, open yet secure, empty yet rich, surrendered and yet free.

You are part of a universal and timeless story, playing out in your life and time. Your current human struggles are familiar stories, tied to generations past and to come. Everything old is new again. You are everyman and everywoman. And every man and every woman is you.

Your personal development along the way has ripened you. No one and nothing human is really foreign to you anymore. Everywhere you know kinship: the child and the crone, the retarded and the genius, the ugly and the beautiful, the sinner and the saint. No emotion or quality is foreign: love, hate, creativity, destruction, sloth, earnestness, pretense, genuineness, enlightenment, stupidity, refinement and vulgarity. You know them all and identify with none. This leaves you strangely and wonderfully ecstatic, being all and being none, all at once.

Life is metaphor, creation showing you endless facets of your radiant self. A starry night feels like home. The tree branch fragrant with blossoms is your spirit's delicate sweetness. The rain rushing down a waterspout moves with intensity, down to the low places, and, finally, to the ocean itself. The water's urgency is familiar, like your own heart, restless and seeking, and finally finding repose.

Your own life is a metaphor of the infinite Ground of Being in time, arising, unfolding and returning back onto itself. You have known this cycle many times in your life, having many beginnings, unfoldings and endings. You have had these for yourself and been them for others. What you mostly identify with now is this Ground of Being. Your unfoldings are part of this greater unfolding. That you are part of Spirit in time makes you incredibly happy.

You know that this one Ground of Being is the one Self in us all. It is the Christ, the Buddha, the Tao, the Great Spirit, the Friend, the Presence. Each of us is one Spirit manifesting in time. Only this Identity gives meaning to all your other identities. Within it all your stops along the way in the spiral of life have their contented place. Without this unifying, boundless center that you are, these limited identities would not fulfill. Their imperfections would rip your boundless being apart in bitterness and remorse.

Only Spirit is perfect in this life and only Spirit lasts. No matter where you are in the spiral of life, you only need to remember that you are also Spirit manifesting in time, to return to your original joy! You are the place where the flow of being is emerging, manifesting and moving on, endlessly forming and transforming. You are like a waterwheel, a wheel of life.

89 Conscient Focus
Open Focus

You have tamed your wandering mind. In the beginning it was headstrong and scattered. You learned to concentrate, to set goals and achieve them and to create a successful life. Deeper awareness beckoned to be integrated into your understanding. You opened your eyes to worlds within, more subtle and powerful, of inspiration, passion, symbolism and meaning. Worlds without became more complex, with much that was contradictory, hidden, compromised, unknown and no longer you. Finally a personal freedom within you became more real. This personal freedom center gave you the choice of observing all things, but not being pulled in by all things.

You are both centered and open in your focus. At the center you are at peace, secure and free. Your freedom allows you your emptiness, your receptivity, your openness. Your personal liberation that allows your open focus is referred to in many traditions. Philosophy calls it going beyond or transcending or freedom. Spirituality calls it God. In the Taoist ox-herding pictures, this personal mastery of your self is pictured as taming an ox. First the ox is wild. Then you tame it. Finally, there is no ox and no you in the picture, just an empty circle. In the final picture you happily return to the marketplace with helping hands, finding Buddha Nature everywhere.

Your open mind is strong now, made so by the disciplined practices that have brought you this far. Your inner freedom gives you many choices for focus. You can concentrate on one thing. You can practice insight meditation, learning from the ongoing flow of your awareness. You can enter altered states. You can bring inner and outer worlds together through symbols and stories. You may choose to become one with the object of your focus, be it your beloved, your work, nature, an inner character or God. You can focus on your breath in order to stop thoughts, and access a wordless, deeper consciousness, that brings first equanimity, and then joy. You can be in effortless clear awareness. You, in your personal freedom center, choose.

Open focus is not about "coming to terms with things as they are." Things are as they are and you are open to the fact that it is so. Whether inner or outer, personal or social, there is simply your open, pure consciousness. It is as though your focus is that of Spirit in time, for the moment, beyond your personal concerns, not limited by your personal self. You participate in a larger, universal mind, one shared by all. Your personal freedom is strong enough and stable enough to experience this wider access, while maintaining your capacity to switch back to your everyday personal life.

With this eye of Spirit you often perceive things not known from your merely personal life. You may intuit the inner life of plants, of animals, of minerals. Dreams may give you insights and experiences reserved for shamans, foreign cultures, gifted scientists or mystic saints. You may remember things long past. You may know the future. You sense what people are thinking. You might do remote viewing, seeing from afar. You see auras, perceive subtle energies and are able to engage them. You may do healings. You may even perceive additional worlds beyond our familiar time and space dimension.

All of this open focus has given you unusual experiences, those shared with mystics and visionaries. That you know such mystery and beauty that is beyond words to express, moves you to deep respect and awe. This open focus allows you to access the sacred, beyond all conditioning. The personal and the universal are yours. This small self, maturing into open focus, is capable of infinite richness.

90 Conscient Relationships
Interconnected

You began your relationships needy, naïve and narcissistic. Gradually you learned to be less self-centered, and to take others more seriously, taking in their point of view. Because you could let others in, you found success in love and work. You learned, by and by, to be more genuine in your relating, expressing yourself more honestly, but with both tact and precision, as needed. Now, relating is less about your personal relationships, and more about interconnection everywhere. You live within a great web of interconnected being. Relating is not so much about coming together. Relating is more about realizing that we are already one, and have always been so.

Your most important relationship is to a grand Presence within and sensed everywhere. You know this Presence. It is the spirit that rises up in your creative, contented, and quiet times that makes living joyous and rich. Its absence makes life mean and stingy. This Presence is immediate, here, now. This presence makes relating to everyone keen, fresh, effortless, eager, direct, playful, tender, open and generous.

This Presence within your being flows into every connection. Who you relate to doesn't determine how you relate. With such a Beloved already in your soul, there is only kinship and generosity everywhere. No one is a stranger. There is no friend or enemy, no American and Arab, no have and have-not, no left wing or right wing, poor or rich, aggressor or victim. There is only one streaming love. When living in this streaming richness, it is of no consequence if the other is moving toward you or away from you. You are already in the resurrection place, beyond personal concerns.

This is the love of God lovers, intoxicated, looking crazy. This love is steadfast, no matter what the news is of the outside world. Bewildered with love, burning within, these God lovers know the source of their unshakable joy, and so only relate with the abandoned generosity of Spirit's gifts. Only a boundless, grand relationship within could make this crazy-looking love without seem sane.

This richness of Spirit that is yours creates a mirror. The fresh, open and radiant Self that streams from your face is the mirror. In it others remember their own shining, radiant Self. Lovers shine this way, whether sitting together in awe-struck silence, or dancing for joy.

You also mirror others by giving them the gift of themselves, reflecting back to them their feelings, thoughts, behaviors and connections. The genuine empathy and compassion strengthen your own selfless clarity and the other person's sense of self and make you one.

You are free to do this loving over and over, connected, as you are, to an infinite source within. You are mirror to the world, and the world finds itself known through you. And so you bring love everywhere, wrapping all in love, with no need for recognition. Your treasure lies elsewhere. Everyone for you is a gem, polished by your love, and treasured by your selfless heart.

You are Spirit in time. In time Spirit ebbs and flows, in endless streams of rising and falling, growth and stability, struggle and resolution. Yet all the while there remains within you the abiding, of you and the Beloved. It remains through loss, betrayal, grief or the coming apart from another for a greater good. You may forget Spirit's presence and be thrown into suffering. But Spirit never forgets you. It is true and constant.

If this infinite love has come to you, make off with it at once. Elope with the bride or bridegroom of your soul. If it has not yet arrived, clear a space. Empty yourself of your important, busy, little thinking self. Slow down. Sit. Embrace solitude. Be quiet. Be open. Listen. Wait. Be ready to receive. Awe and gratitude will wash over you, as the Beloved of your soul appears.

What is unnatural in ordinary love is reasonable inside this Spirit place. The richness and beauty of the Beloved is already glowing inside your chest. Love or lack of it doesn't apply here. Separation and need and judgment exist in time. In timelessness there is only this one, streaming, interconnected love. From this deeper, universal place, we are all looking out at each other with the same interconnected eye. We're all loving each other with the same throbbing heart.

91 Conscient Emotions
Well-Being

Your emotional life has served you well, with anger, fear, need and greed protecting you, when you needed it from a scary world, helping you to survive physically and emotionally. You slowly learned skills beyond these self-centered emotional protections, gaining enough self-control and savvy to become successful in the larger community. Eventually you gained insight into your feelings, learning to name them, tame them and express them with appropriate tact and honesty. Now emotions come and go, like familiar old acquaintances. You mindfully pay attention to the emotional stream of feelings toward things within and without. Your mindfulness buffers you from the river's incessant movement and gives you a peaceful perch of well-being on the edge from which you observe.

Mindfulness is the observer in you that is free. Mindfulness is a choice that you make over and over. It maintains your well-being, and keeps you free of outer events overly affecting you. Mindfulness gives you freedom to laugh, or to see things from a different perspective. Mindfulness gives you a base from which to bring forth kindness, nurturing, patience and love. This inner freedom gives you hope that problems can be overcome, balance achieved and connections strengthened.

And there is well-being that is not your choice, but comes to you unbidden. This majesty breaks you open to awe and joy. Fear, shame and urgency are from another time and another place. They are gone, replaced by personal worthiness, universal love and effortless flow. This majestic well-being from within is the basis of our human dignity and maybe of all ethics, relating and probably even civilization itself.

Flow is suffused with quiet excitement and deep fulfillment, as you work effortlessly and well. You experience entrainment, as your rhythms come into sync with other natural rhythms around you. You experience deep contentment, delight and happiness in being in natural harmony all around.

Gratitude and humility no longer are choices or practices. They are natural sweetness pouring out of your awe-struck, love-filled, broken-open heart. Your well-being is so deep, so secure, that openness to others is inevitable.

Out of your well-being flows unconditional love for all, affirming goodness where you find it, and moving, in compassion, toward well-being everywhere. Imagine our lives if we met others in such heartfelt empathy, no matter where they are in the spiral of life. All would be streaming life, open, respectful, honest and moving toward reconciliation. In our lives we would manifest in time the deep well-being we already have within our own selves.

92 Conscient Ethics
Universal Compassion, Justice & Service

Your ethics began as a child. First, right behavior was what you could get away with. By and by such self-absorbed actions were replaced by knowledge of the ways of the world. You became a successful adult, being shaped by much reward and punishment. Your own self-confidence grew as you reflected on your experiences over time. This deepened self trust led you to live by your own personal integrity. Being true to yourself required ongoing personal discipline and ever more refined personal mastery. You experienced the sweetness of inner freedom and personal wholeness. This brought you to the very source of right behavior itself, your own original Self. Out of this rich, bountiful Source flows the bountiful stream of universal compassion, justice and service.

It takes much inner strength and even courage to maintain contact with your inner richness. You must make it a priority to stay close your source of inner goodness. You return to it in your solitude and practices, renewing your weary, dried up soul, becoming green again and ripe, a true human being.

Personal injuries are dissolved in this healing place. Ugliness falls away. Laughter rises up from your liberation. You see the self-important, illusory seriousness with which you take the world, and you get the big joke being played on us all. We are struggling, while we are already free. We seem separate, yet we have always

233

been together. We feel inadequate, yet we are already infinitely rich.

Your open heart receives all beings, people, animals, plants, even the living planet and the cosmos itself. Your heart is filled with simplicity and childlike innocence. Compassion effortlessly streams through you to yourself and to all. Your own flaws and mistakes and personal evil burn away in the presence of the abiding goodness that fills you up. Those who do wrong know not what they do.

You are ready again and again to be of service, to strive for justice, to practice generosity and to live in love. Personal justice for yourself is not something you cling to. If you receive injustice, you return justice. If you are slapped on one cheek, you may even turn the other cheek. Why? Because the insult helps to break open your hard, time-bound self, clinging to the things of time in order to feel whole. Turning the other cheek helps you to strip away your needy, demanding, puffed up, self-importance. You want to be purified more and more of your own limiting little self that readily finds insult. Difficulties may also make the return home all the sweeter.

Self-centered anger, control, greed, hatred, injustice, lies and lust are all unethical behavior. They arise out of the misguided ways of creatures in time. Imagine a world where we live from our inner richness streaming into the world. Anger becomes kind. Self-righteous rage melts through thoughtful, attitude-shifting humor into compassion. Power serves the greater good. Imagine living more simply, so you might share more and others might have more. Imagine meeting hatred with a consistent, abiding love. Imagine injustice being solved with equal rights and opportunities. Imagine simple honesty replacing lies. Imagine love without betrayal or possession. Imagine a conscient life of kindness, service and justice, streaming from a full-up heart.

93 Conscient Awareness
Spirit and Being

You have seen life with the eye of your needy self, the eye of physical and emotional survival. You then learned to focus, with sharp logic and heartfelt connection, the eyes of mind and heart. With the eye of soul you began to open up to more subtle realms, and experienced their power to deeply move you. And now, with the eye of Spirit, you are poised to see infinity shining everywhere.

What was reasonable before is turned on its head through the eye of Spirit. You live in two worlds now, one as a time space creature, and in the other, as a resurrection being. It is a life hard to describe directly. You reason now with an expanded logic, the logic of the mystic, of paradox. You value the koan, whose non-logic shuts the mind down so that in the gap of no thinking, you can open up to original, wordless awareness and to joy.

Images abound. Out of the mud arises the lotus. The old crone inside feels like a beautiful young bride. The old man inside knows he is strong and handsome. The cripple runs. In nothing you find wealth. In giving you receive. Emptiness fills you up. Silence pours harmonies. You make progress by waiting. The bawdy gives rise to the sublime. Your shadow life reveals the treasure. Suffering and love are partners. You know space without boundaries, time without movement. You disappear and you become everything. In leaving the world you enrich the world.

Your weeping, grateful being eagerly lives as Spirit in time. Your little self has found its fullness. You were made for this joy. There is only the present, the flow of being, rich, gorgeous and ineffable.

Intoxication pours in. Your awareness is that of a God-annihilated creature. You are God-intoxicated.

Your Beloved cannot be seen, yet everywhere wordless metaphors reveal the Beloved, who is everywhere and who we are. Something of the Beloved is revealed in the shining of green leaves, the earthy smell of baking bread, the soothing sound of running water, the union of our loving, the restoration in our sleep, the adventures in our dreaming, the joy in our work, the hope in our losses, and the renewal in our suffering. You trust this Beloved to take your life.

Fear of the ecstatic is not of the Friend. No need to rave either. You are a real human being now. No more need for preaching, for theory, for art, for distractions, for recognition. These may have brought you this far. Now they fall away, giving way to direct realization of your timeless being. You have been to the mountain. A thread of remembering keeps you connected to your resurrection place, as you go about your daily business in the spiral of life.

There is only the endless return to the Friend, sitting in the Presence, finding comfort, knowing wealth. Blissed-out, awe struck, inspired and enchanted, you amble about in time, your living a playful delight, practicing gentleness, giving comfort and making peace. You, a poor and obscure creature, born of dust and returning to dust, are regal in your natural wealth, loving more, doing less, and delighting in your being. You stay connected to the One who moves through us all in the spiral of life, there from the beginning, uniting us all, now and now and now.

94 Conscient Wisdom
Direct Experience of Timeless Spirit

Your wisdom began in the limits of your small self, aware mostly of its personal pain and suffering. You found some answers to coping with pain and suffering, conventional ones that others gave you. You eventually found your own personal meaning, through your own reflections and personal honesty. And now your search for wisdom has taken you to where you have been drawn your entire life. Your conscient wisdom connects you directly to timeless Spirit itself.

You don't need to search anymore for a source of deep peace, wild generosity, hilarious joy or irrational love. Out of you, with freedom and ease, they flow. Your regular practices, to simply be, to center yourself, to concentrate, to gain insight, enter a state of grace or to embrace Spirit, link you back, again and again, to Source. You are freed from the meager resources of time. You live, in this very moment of now, in the vast richness of the timeless present, where eternity itself resides, and it is yours.

Small egos are scattered by the majesty of this universal way of being. It may seem a simple and foolish wisdom to the uninitiated, finding majesty and joy in this renunciation of separateness, of self-consciousness, of fear or urgency. Your love-quickened, surrendered soul has no need of fear or judgment or hurry.

There is no how or why, just the ecstatic *ahhhhh* flowing out of your melted, open, weeping, ecstatic Self. Peaceful is the river that flows through you in pure silence, murmuring its sweetest song of emptiness, soothing you with its delicate presence, teaching you its open secret, breaking open your frozen heart, like the ecstatic joy of lovers coming together.

Resurrection in time is lived with full clarity. You understand how time and timelessness coexist, looping back and forth onto each other in endless delight. Gratitude fills you as you participate in this sacred loop between worlds. In this looping back and forth between worlds, you are held quivering, intensely energized, yet perfectly still.

Out of the mists of timeless being, hovering over the waters of your living self, you shape the creation of your own life, called forth by the breath of your own struggles and purpose. Intention is a portal between time and the timeless. Your intentions shape-shift the infinite possibilities of the infinite void. Your direction is put out with confidence and trust, as effortless as the space between your breaths, the gap between your words. It is put out into the void of no-thing-ness. By intention you shape-shift the manifestation of the greater reality in your life.

World events are understood quickly, by your wise heart, recognizing, with wordless sympathy, the frailties of human nature, as it flails about in time, causing suffering and pain all around.

Imagine a world where more and more persons live this state of being that we call "God." It is a place neuroscientists find within our brains, accessible by all, not only by the blessed or the privileged or "believers." You, and everyone, can access the infinite within your own being. Invited or not, timeless Spirit goes about its business of enlivening us, renewing us, deepening clarity, anchoring stability, celebrating fluidity and generating love. And

239

yes, by our innerwork practices, we strengthen its presence in our lives.

You, who are in love with the Infinite loop from time to the beyond and back again. You bring back into time all the gifts of Spirit for creatures of time. You bring the peace that passes understanding. You give life to enfolded harmonies everywhere, with your clear, awakened heart. You live the serenity of love, the very love that is embracing you, enfolding you, and by your intention, flowing out, through you, to the world. You and timeless Spirit are one in your love for the creatures of time.

Conscient Social Development

95 Conscient Family
Family of Origin, Committed Relationships and Support Circles

Being family is living life at its source. You live with others in circles of support to generate and nourish and celebrate life itself. For you this is the very work of creation, of the divine. It is not just about you, your progeny and your heritage. It is about loving life, supporting it, and giving it wing. Past and future generations ripple out from you and your moment in time, rippling out from the unfolding of your interconnected life.

Your family values are idealistic. You let life flow freely and in supporting the best in others, you bring out the best in yourself. Your life and the lives of others thrive. You live from the highest ideals. You balance freedom and support. Self-expression and the greater good come together. You value communication, consistency, commitment, fairness, honesty, unconditional acceptance and respect for the personal dignity of all, including children. Even if things aren't going well, your ideals are challenged to rise to the occasion. In your values you find inner direction, strength and dignity. Your intent is consistent support and connection through good times and bad. Troubled family life may emerge far stronger because you give your unfailing support. Security, enjoyment and warmth allow individuals to thrive.

The greater good of your group informs the decisions you make. Planning helps provide a secure and serene stage for the family as a whole, and for the individuals within it to thrive. Your planning aims for balance, order and memorable enjoyment. Days flow freely and all unfolds naturally. Giving and receiving take their turn in you and others in this supportive and free way to live. This applies to holidays, get-togethers, estate planning or reunions.

You maintain self-expression by freely expressing yourself, calmly, respectfully, without self-consciousness. You have nothing to prove. Your self-expression delights in its natural style. You take joy in others freely expressing themselves as well. Noticing subtle changes in maturing self-expression in your family makes you happy! Alone and yet together, all members freely co-exist to hear and be heard, not, "to be seen and not heard."

Your family of origin gives you connections to generations past and future. Remembering and responsibility prevail. The ancestors are a part of your life, respected for their distinctive contributions and acknowledged for their challenging limitations. Future generations are anticipated as recipients of your life choices and self-expression.

You enter into marriage and committed relationship for mutual support, supporting who each most needs to be. Love provides abiding support of each other's freedom. In choosing love, you support your partner's deepest desires, while finding your own unfolding strengthened. Such interactive intimacy melts your separateness, creating enchantment between you, and may move you into awestruck gratitude for what you share. Your personal self thrives, while living out of this abiding commitment and enriching spirit. You choose, and even plan, to do regularly what deepens your relationship. You seek to deepen your love, and then widen the circle of love to others. Unfailing support begins at home and encircles the world.

Unfailing support that can be relied on is how you do family. You are your brother's keeper, and with luck, they may act as yours as well. You attempt to love all equally and fairly. There is always forgiveness for wrongs, and acceptance of others as they are. In the most inclusive sense, family extends to "all my relatives," all nations, all creeds and all creatures.

96 Conscient Politics
Personal Rights, Public Good, Public Safety and Public Office

Politics, the art of the possible, is at its zenith! You are undeterred by seeing politics used for the special interests of appalling personal greed and power. As a politician you are an idealist. You are a visionary. Your special interests are the interests of all. Your visionary ideals are forever falling short of realization, but not your commitment to them. The planet is a long way from inclusive liberty, justice and opportunity for all, but these values prevail, as you support nonviolent means to achieve these universal equal rights. You will not be moved. You are undaunted in your commitment to your ideals.

The profound disillusionment that people have with politics is because they care so deeply about justice, and see it violated regularly by clever propaganda, corruption, ignorance and mediocrity. People don't lack idealism. Small minded politicians betray the common good.

Equal opportunity in work, equal education and equal fairness under the law are still ideals in a democratic society. Individual dignity and universal brotherhood are the basis of political action. These ideals are the basis from which to strive for a compassionate society of freedom for all.

Let culture everywhere celebrate this freedom of the human spirit, and its constant yearning to surpass itself. Happiness and human perfection cannot be guaranteed, but the right to pursue them can. We love the homeland and are generous with the dispossessed. We strive to treat all equally, even in a society riddled with class differences.

Political values are always clarified by looking at what works for the greater common good. Principles of universal fairness are timeless in their goodness and inclusiveness.

Government resources are a safety network against the deepest anxieties of survival for the frail and the elderly and those down on their luck. A system of care for the poor has always been a hallmark of a civilized society.

Conscient politicians support the ideals of healthy, nonviolent conflict resolution as a means to address injustices. Violence has many causes. Some are in society. Some are in the human heart. Social justice is the work of us all. So is the cleansing of the human heart. We recognize the seductive power of war, and instead, turn swords into plowshares.

Criminals not only need to pay their dues to society. They also need forgiveness and opportunities for making amends, for learning compassion for their victims, and for rebuilding their lives. Conditions out of which crime flourishes need to boldly addressed. Peace begins with justice. And equal opportunity.

Politics is not about achieving a perfect world. Politics is about working for it without fail. Your idealistic work, whether as a volunteer or a political professional, may kindle a fire of inspiration in other human hearts as well. You give voice to your idealism, not because it makes a good "sound bite," but because working toward the universal good makes you a great politician.

97 Conscient Religion/Arts
Art, Philosophy, Psychology and Religion

Sacred space is yours, "whose center is everywhere and whose circumference is nowhere." You may feel the pressures of responder neediness, or the stress of conformity, or the urge to genuine personal expression, or the yearning to live with flow and entrainment. No matter where you are in the spiral of life, it does not fully define you. You create sacred space as you remember your link to timelessness in time, wherever you are in the spiral of life.

Beyond all ordinary logic or conditioning, there rises up in you an indifference to the corruption time brings. You are not your losses, your suffering or your aging self. Your ineffable, true Self, that has been with you your entire life, is always the same, and creates sacred space wherever you are aware of it. You sit in this simple state of grace, this ground of being, forever young. You experience the limitless richness and beauty that you are. You do practices to return to direct experience of your timeless Self, ineffable, indefinable, boundless, blissful, bringing you deepest peace.

Right behavior flows habitually out of you, long disciplined as you are, over the years, to do the right thing. Now this right behavior couldn't be any other way. Your transformed, clear self lives in love. Understanding, compassion, humor, kindness and the greater good inform all your doings. You instinctively practice the golden rule, doing to others as you want done to you. And your practice of compassion starts with compassion for yourself.

Spirit renews your inner richness. You are forever new. Out of you flows an open, deeply loving connection to life. There are no friends, no enemies, no believers and no unbelievers. There is just the one Spirit flowing, uniting all.

You select art with care. You choose movies, theatre and literature for their insight in overcoming the limits of the human condition. Any art form must break open your small self, melt your frozen heart, inspire your weary self, and transport you into awe, thus, linking you back to your original Self.

Various growth traditions may attract you to join their community, valuing the interconnectedness belonging brings, even while feeling you have already "arrived." You may join, knowing you are already kin. Your exaltation knows no bounds as you join others in praise of what you together hold most sacred.

The practices and rituals within community may generate synergy for you. You may be socially invigorated as you explore, celebrate or experience beauty, truth and goodness with others.

Yet, wherever anyone is growing is spiritual, their growth expressing spiritual freedom to always go beyond their present, limited, conditioned self. A growth tradition may be religious or ethical or educational or artistic in nature, each supporting one's dynamic place in the spiral of life.

The ineffable, the mysterious, being moved to awe, to rapture, to love, to service, these are the highest realms of being. You know the path. Finding it and being faithful to it have brought you to this point. Now your desire is to stay on the journey that already feels like home, so transported are you by its beauty, truth, goodness and love. You experience joy wherever you see Spirit taking form in time. With the eye of Spirit, you see that Spirit is taking form everywhere.

98 Conscient Sex/Closeness
Eroticism, Sex, Connectedness, Love, Communication,
Masculine And Feminine Orientation

Your connecting is most alive, on fire from within. You are not looking for anyone to complete you. Connecting has entered the realm of the spiritual, the unseen. As with the mystics, you are enlivened with an inexpressible vitality. Your connecting to others is now a celebration of life itself.

This conscient, juicy, erotic joy of living can take place in even mundane, everyday circumstances. It has a sense of now, of being fully present, with a freewheeling lack of self-consciousness. Give and take flow; playfulness prevails.

It comes from the deep place within, where there is no "you and me." There is only the oneness with each other and its attending joys. This rising up may be felt, as if a third presence has come to join you. It seems beyond time, feeling magical and enchanting, like a gift of grace. This enchantment is intoxicating to you, irresistible, ineffable and intense. No longer are your connections between one little-self and another little-ego-self. In your relating, you are experiencing what it means to be immersed, in time, in the timeless Spirit of Love. If two or more come together in peace and love, the unseen arrives with its gifts.

This space between is full of paradox. A felt connection between you and another enlivens and unifies. Yet you both stay free. You are vulnerable and open. Yet you are secure and self-contained.

Your truest self is celebrated. Yet you are celebrating the other. The connection is unifying. But it is non-possessive. It is expansive, but not annihilating. Two or more become one. Yet you remain separate. Sometimes there is happy, festive and joyous noise. Other times there may be a wordless, awestruck, revelatory silence.

Sexuality is especially powerful in its ability to take you out of the ordinary. Body, mind and spirit are all brought into sharp focus and unified, resulting in transcending pleasure. Lovers are released from the ordinary. They are released from their separateness. This is a heightened state of being where all is physically and spiritually intense.

In lovemaking, lovers are broken open. They flow into each other. One lover fills the other lover's soul. They enter a realm sublime and ecstatic. Loving unifies, with lovers tending to each other's pleasure and surrendering at the same time. The sacred is invoked in this sacrament of sex. The bed becomes the sacred grove.

All of this takes acute skills of rapport in reading other people's cues, even the most subtle. Regular rituals help to encourage this intimacy. These rituals keep relating secure and fresh, rituals such as regular talks, walks, romantic "nights out," "date nights" at home, getaways, shared spiritual practices, retreats and renewals.

Your connections with others celebrate differences and their distinctive gifts. You find a way to unite, not divide. You balance boundaries of self-care with loving another, focusing on the greater good that supports us all. There is no possessiveness and no power grabbing. You let things flow naturally. Even one person in this unifying mode can change the dynamics of an entire group.

The inner world between you and another is ineffable, unique and creative. You encourage it by being deeply present, practicing attentive, receptive and unconditional love. Unseen forces come to your aid, giving substance to your intentions, and helping you all live well in the world together.

99 Conscient Social Situations
Food, Shelter, Clothing, Cyberspace, Society and Time

Where you live and how you live no longer identifies you. You now identify with the world. You are the world and the world is you. A deep awareness that all is interconnected creates this expansive identity. It makes you feel responsible for life, makes you feel that what you do matters, that somehow every choice you make has implications, that they somehow tweak the universal energy field.

You come to your possessions, your home and to social situations with a personal freedom. You don't need to personally possess or control these things. You already are one with the source of possessions and life itself. Everything is metaphor and reveals yet another quality of your soul and of your Beloved.

Your behavior in what you eat and buy and use has an eye to interconnectedness and well-being everywhere. You choose products with the larger picture in mind: health, pollution, sustainability and humane working conditions. You patronize stores that provide "fair trade" products, local, organic produce, or support indigenous businesses. Voluntary simplicity makes for a lighter footprint on the planet and a more restful home.

For some, food may be simple and is not fussed over. For others, food is chosen to be fresh and appealing, feeding body and spirit. Social and personal get-togethers celebrate the joy of living. All are made to feel included. Generosity prevails. Drug and alcohol use enhance, not detract from, your well-being. The clothes you wear may express simplicity or your inner beauty and celebrate it.

Timeless values are enhanced as you live with taste, beauty and quality that nourish your soul. Your pets are honored for their share in universal consciousness, often with distinctive sensitivities.

Your home reflects connections to your interests and perhaps your ancestors. The home itself has a history and is full of interconnections. You don't so much own things, as care for them, passing them on to others. The same stewardship is felt for your neighborhood and for the land.

Education serves equal opportunity, personal excellence and heartfelt living. Health care is for all, reflecting basic human dignity. Service to the community motivates your involvement. Every action you take reflects your universal kinship with the planet and your society.

Time is mostly the present moment, and you flow easily in it. This effortlessness of the present moment is an experience of ongoing, contented, living freedom. Leisure and work balance each other, with a yin yang touch of each in the other.

The interconnectedness of all things sometimes finds you pondering time and timelessness in things. Things around you have a history, sometimes millions and billions of years old. A simple possession in your home took many hands to bring to you, perhaps from around the world. Cyberspace mimics the universality of the connections in which we already live and move and have our being.

To conclude by linking all of these social connections to their ultimate, we might say that in the beginning there was the void out of which all things came. This matrix of being is the ultimate link in social connections. The Ground of Being is you home, as surely as your four walls.

100 Conscient Work
*Money, Livelihood, Hobbies, Special Interests, Daily Routines &
Useful Activity*

Work has become timeless flow for you. You are inspired, but not manic. You are disciplined, but not burdened. You nurture the spirits of those around you, but are not drained. You work toward an ideal society, knowing there can only be perfection within Spirit.

How you achieve such a balance between doing and being reflects your lifelong journey toward greater self-understanding, self-mastery and effortless skills in your chosen field. You are doing right livelihood, what really matters to you. Your work may express your stage in life, your personal self-expression as well as universal values of timeless goodness. Money is less about greed, and more about an exchange of energy and love.

Your inner life provides ongoing inspiration to which you can return for refreshment and renewed energy. Returning to your inner self for renewal keeps your spirit fresh and clear. You return again and again, keeping yourself anchored in goodness, despite encountering cynicism and corruption and whatever gives rise to them.

Your workplace may be secular or spiritual, but your intention is to do your best in loving service, no matter what the work. It may be family, politics, church, the arts, learning, personal development, science, the market place, or helping others link back to their original Self.

Your work is as much mindful process as it is productivity. You act with a sense of flow, that is, effortless activity that slightly challenges your abilities. Your work engages you. It may be simple work, but you are present to it, one with it. Your work may be complex and challenging, yet your focus is organized and your engagement slow, orderly and entrained. You are immersed in your tasks, working in a self-directed, easy and effortless manner.

Accomplishment may matter, yet you don't push the process. You are the servant to whatever it takes to see a project through. Quietly dynamic and effortless, you are a calm in the midst of activities. Your deepest inspirations within may find kindred spirits for joint efforts in committed, inspired work. You may experience the energizing dynamics of synergy, where the effects of working together are multiplied, where one and one are more than two.

How you work increases the cohesiveness of all parts of your life. You find that your accomplishments, large and small, all come together into a unified whole. Mindful, flowing and entrained, your work style moves toward simplicity in the midst of complexity.

Your behavior is trustworthy, because you value selfless consistency, honesty and cooperation. Truthfulness and fairness are the basis for doing the right thing. The truth is spoken simply and kindly. This applies to the boss, your fellow workers, your clients and the larger world.

Spiritual conversion may shift your personal ambitions. It did for St. Augustine, who found once coveted influence in high places disgusting, as he discovered the gentleness and beauty of the world within. The Sufi poet Rumi tells of a mystically oriented father, who left his inheritance to his laziest son. God's hand works everywhere, and the father figured that his least ambitious son would have the patience needed to open his inner eye. He would receive without possessing and so stay free.

There is work and there is simple being. To bring work and simple being together is an ancient ideal, urging effortless activity or creative quiet in all you do. And so, it is possible that you may bring together all that you are, inner and outer, body, mind and heart, soul and Spirit.

Appendices

Appendix 1: Glossary

Active Imagination Using simple imagining or movement or acting out or drawing or writing to amplify impressions received from innerwork symbols, body symptoms or work and relationship experiences in the world

Addiction Self destructive or ineffective behavior

Awareness What you are conscious of through the body, mind or experience in the world; Through 4 Levels of Development: From The Merely Physical & Self-Centered, To The Eyes Of Mind & Heart, To Soul, To Spirit And Being

Body The physical, eye of body, 1st stage of human development, non-aware ego/no ego, focused on physical and emotional survival

Butterfly Effect The influence of a small change rippling through a larger system

Closeness A kinship feeling, or an erotic binding connection

Co-dependency Relying on another to feel good about yourself and then trying to control that person for your own needs

Collective Unconscious Patterns within the person that are below consciousness and found in every culture and every human being; these patterns can be of behavior, beliefs, emotions, symbols, body responses and energy fields, reflecting various levels of subtlety

Conformist The second of four levels of personal development, usually young adulthood, emphasizing taking the role of the other, in order to successfully live cooperatively in both work and love

Conscient The fourth and highest stage of personal development, usually in mature adulthood, emphasizing the subtlety and interconnectedness of all things, leading to universal, timeless, Self-realization and all its gifts of Spirit in time

Defense A natural, psychological pattern, usually unconscious, to protect one's sense of self from threat, through denial, projection, wishful thinking, dissociation, etc.

Deferred gratification Putting off enjoying yourself now for a greater good in the future

Denial A natural, spontaneous defense against some threat to one's sense of self, which refuses to admit the problem

Dissociation A natural, spontaneous defense against a threat to one's sense of self, which cuts off feelings or experiences from consciousness as they are happening

Eastern Growth traditions from Asian cultures such as India, China and Japan, including, but not limited to, Hinduism, Buddhism, Taoism, etc.

Ego Who you think you are at any given time; a healthy sense of self; the conformist, 2nd stage of human development, combining masculine side of knowing and achievement (mind) with the feminine side of belonging (heart)

Emotional Intelligence The ability to name and control emotions

Emotions An instinctive, natural response of feelings to situations, giving you instant feedback and guidance to act; Through 4 Levels of Development: From Anger, Fear, Greed & Need, To Self Control, To Recognizing And Expressing Emotions, To Well-Being

Enmeshment Emotional entanglement, relying on another for personal well-being, with little sense of personal boundaries between oneself and the other

Entrainment Your activities coming into synchronization with other natural rhythms, creating a cohesive present, slow, orderly and enjoyable

Erotic A felt sense of connection

Ethics A code of right and wrong behavior that guides your choices in word, thought and deed, leading to self-control, social conscience, and inner freedom; Through 4 Levels of Development: From Getting Away With Things, To Reward & Punishment, To Personal Integrity, To Universal Compassion, Justice & Service

Evil Whatever separates or causes pain or harm to yourself or others, open to many interpretations

Family The people we identify with, who provide us a feeling of belonging, of kinship, and mutual support; (Family Of Origin, Committed Relationships And Support Circles)

Feminine and Masculine Two sides of human personality in both men and women: the masculine, achieving side and the feminine, belonging side

Flow Effortless activity that slightly challenges your abilities

Focus The ability to direct your attention in a chosen way; Through 4 Levels of Development: From Scattered To Intensifying Concentration, To Integrating, To Opening Focus

God Universal quickening or ground of being of all; beyond limits of time, yet manifested in time; energizing and informing all personal growth stages and their development; consciously and directly realized in the fourth or conscient stage of development; referred to as Essential Nature, Ground of Being, Ultimate Reality, God, Father, Spirit, Great Mother, The Friend, The Inner Beloved, Self, Tao, Buddha, Christ, Divine, Nature, the Presence, the Quantum Field, Reality, Timeless Being, etc.; Conscious connection to God is experienced as a connection to a conscious Presence of abiding love and knowing, bringing freedom from personal limitations and associated suffering, providing an interconnectedness of all things, in time and timelessness, leading to awe, well-being, deep peace, love, joy, contentment, sweetness, constancy and other gifts of Spirit, and feeling like personal liberation, waking up, coming home, having arrived and knowing what you were made for.

Growth Traditions   Bodies of teachings about the nature of human beings and how to live well; five major traditions are: Judeo/Christian/Muslim, Eastern, Indigenous, psychosocial and holistic science

Heart   Belonging, the eye of heart, the 2nd stage of human-development, ego identity, focused on kinship and erotic connection

Holistic Science   A complimentary or alternative approach to the physical sciences that integrates body, mind, soul and spirit levels

Hologram   A 3D image, capable of showing a part and the whole at the same time, showing different images from different perspectives

Identity   Who you are over a lifetime; how others know you, or how you see yourself; Through 4 Levels of Development: From Self-Protective, To Conventional Roles and Rules, To Authentic, To Transpersonal

Indigenous   Growth traditions of native peoples such as shamanic, Wicca, Native American and Aboriginal; There is a strong emphasis on relationship to natural forces and inner spheres of reality.

Individualist   The third stage of human development, usually in mid-life adulthood, emphasizing becoming receptive, reflective and real, about how things really are, leading to personal authenticity, creativity, and expanded self-realization, often partnering the individual small self with the higher Self

Innerwork A receptive attention to the three "S's" of awareness: symbols, symptoms and signals;   Innerwork amplifies the **symbols** of dreams, imagination and fantasy, the body **symptoms** of discomfort and spontaneous movement, and work and relationship **signals** of attraction and withdrawal in the world.

Integral Psychology Personal growth through stages of development, in the inner/personal life of mind and behavior, and the outer/social life of culture and social structure. It unifies numerous approaches such as analytical, gestalt, and transpersonal, reflecting the work of Freud, Jung, Kohlberg, Kohut, Loevinger, Maslow, Piaget, and is especially expressed in the synthesis writings of Ken Wilber. Lifewheel makes integral psychology available in easy to read style.

Interdependent Independent, respectful interaction among persons

Intention Aim, goal, target, objective, plan, meaning, purpose

Judeo/Christian/Muslim Traditions of personal growth; each emphasizing the founders' viewpoints, found in their sacred books and institutions. These are sometimes referred to collectively as the Abrahamic tradition.

Level of Development Developing, progressive stages of human beings, from responder to conformist to individualist to conscient

Line of Development A specific area of human potential, the possibilities of which are myriad, eight of which are given in Lifewheel, going through four stages of development

Lifewheel A blend of integral psychology and the perennial philosophy, showing one's inner and outer worlds informed by the Ground of Being and transforming, from needy and non-aware responder (body), to the smart and successful conformist (mind and heart), to receptive, reflective and real individualist (soul), to the conscient, who is conscious, connected, fully mature, and occasionally, even God-intoxicated (Spirit)

These Lifewheel transformation patterns, showing the dynamics of Spirit in time in humans, are common to all growth traditions. Lifewheel provides a hologram, instantly showing your place in the spiral of life, its relation to the whole and to the Ground of Being, informing it all.

Masculine and Feminine Two sides of human personality in both men and women, the masculine, achieving side and the feminine, belonging side

Mind The logical, eye of mind, the 2nd stage of human development, ego identity, focused on rules of logic and use of reason to be smart and successful

Mind's Eye Receptive eye, the eye of soul, that turns inward, experiencing awareness on levels of body, mind, heart, soul and Spirit; giving reflective attention to body symptoms, dream and imagination symbols, as well as work and relationship signals of attraction and repulsion, in order enhance personal awareness and development

Mindfulness Receptive awareness, allowing alert observation, without having to respond

Mirroring Accurately reflecting a person back to themselves with interpretive or summary statements, such as, *You are proud*, or, *You seem upset.*

Motivation A feeling of enthusiasm, a driving reason or intention for doing something; Through 4 Levels of Development: From Non-aware & Needy, To Doing & Belonging, To Individuality, To Beyond Your Personal Self

Narcissism Being self-involved, unable to take another's point of view seriously enough, referencing all back to yourself

Original Self See Self with capital "S"

Paradox A seemingly contradictory statement that rings true, expressing paradoxical thinking, an indication of time and timelessness coming together in conscient level logic

Paranoia An unreasonable fear that others are out to get you in some way

Perennial Philosophy Timeless philosophy, common to most growth traditions, teaching that there is a universal Ground of Being in which we all participate, and it is a part of being human, being one's core center or Self. It both informs evolution in time, and is beyond the limits of time and space. This Ground of Being acts as a matrix to existence, being constant, conscious and interconnected to all. It does not end for the individual at the body's death. This Ground of Being is understood variously as Buddha Nature, God, the Great Spirit, quantum energy field, Reality, Self, the Tao, universal consciousness, and so on and is consciously known in the conscient level of being.

Politics The art of balancing personal rights and power with public good and government; (Personal Rights, Personal Power, Public Good, Public Safety & Public Office)

Pre-ego Responder level of development, lacking normal, conformist, adult self-development

Primitive thinking A childish, ineffective way of wishful thinking, to get what you want or need

Projection A natural, psychological defense, of seeing the world as we are, reflecting our level of development

Psyche The total life force of an individual, both conscious and unconscious

Psychosocial The collected insights into human behavior from the social science disciplines of psychology and sociology

Reality See God; Infinity looping back and forth between time and timelessness

Regression An earlier, less mature way of handling something, often happening when under stress

Relationships A shared personal space between persons of feeling, behavior and communication; Through 4 Levels of Development: From Being Needy, To Cooperative, To Genuine, To Interconnected

Religion/Arts Institutionalized teachings on the nature of reality and how to live well; (Art, Philosophy, Psychology and Religion)

Repression A natural psychological defense, putting undesirable thoughts and feelings out of our conscious mind

Responder The first stage of human development, usually in childhood and young teenage years, or in needy adults, emphasizing physical and emotional survival, often giving a needy, self-protective and unthinking response to personal needs or to outside influences

Sacred Ordinary experience connected to the timeless, resulting in awe and joy

self The little self with a small "s" is the individual self, experienced as separate, and subject to the laws of time and space

Self The big Self with a capital "S" is the timeless self, the original self, experienced as conscious and interconnected, and going beyond the bounds of time and space

Self-reliance The ability to confidently depend on yourself for your direction and well-being, and not merely relying on instinct and conformity

Sex/Closeness Sex: The urge, the arousal or the bodily expression of sexual energy; Closeness: A kinship feeling, or a felt, binding connection (Eroticism, Sex, Connectedness, Love, Communication, Masculine and Feminine Orientation)

Shadow The dark or bright sides of ourselves that are put out of conscious awareness

Shame A profound sense of personal unworthiness or inadequacy

Signal A message of attraction or discomfort in the world, especially in work and love, and amplified in innerwork to receive guidance in one's life choices

Social Situations Cultural social patterns (Food, Shelter, Clothing, Cyberspace, Society and Time)

Soul One's capacity to be inspirited, to receive inspirations of all sorts; passion; multiple ways of knowing; 3rd stage of human development: ego and Self in partnership, focused on integrating many ways of knowing; the part of an individual that is thought by many to continue in some conscious form after physical death

Space The dimension where time and three-dimensional, physical matter exist, having height, width and depth

Spiral of Life The natural movement of the human spirit in time, coming into being, developing, finding complications, spiraling ahead and falling back, finding one's distinct self-expression and Self-realization, with the quiet center providing a home base of strength and flexibility in a world of constant change

Spirit Timeless Being, without the limits of time and space; 4th stage of human development, enlightened ego in service of Self/No Ego, focused on direct experience of timeless Being

Spiritual The unseen world of Spirit, informing all that is, experienced as subtle, interconnected and liberating, going beyond one's limited self in time and space

Spirituality Practices providing access to the unseen Ground of Being or the conscient level of development; paradox thinking, where the eyes of time and timelessness are both true at once; clear conscient consciousness and connectedness

Symbol An image that unites two or more ways of being, conscious and unconscious, time and timeless, known and unknown, and amplified through associations to receive the "aha" or insight for greater awareness

Symptom A body discomfort, amplified in innerwork, to receive insight into one's self

Synergy Energy results that are greater than the individual parts: "One and one are more than two."

Time A force in space that affects and marks change in physical beings; a system to measure the interval between at least two events in space

Timeless Beyond the bounds of time and place

Transcend Going beyond your present, conditioned, limiting circumstances

"What wants to happen" The unfolding of yourself in the present moment, at the edge of what is and what wants to be, naturally impelling your ongoing development

Wheel of Life A metaphor for yourself in time, of life flowing through you, as you endlessly receive, manifest and let go, moment to moment, with your core self, the quiet center, providing you constancy and joy

Wisdom Attempts to answer life's seemingly insoluble problems, giving meaning to the pain of loss, illness, old age and death; Through 4 Levels of Development: From Painful Personal Boundaries and Suffering, To Conventional Answers, To Inner Meaning, To Direct Experience Of Timeless Spirit

Work Useful activity; (Money, Livelihood, Hobbies, Special Interests, Daily Routines, Useful Activity)

Appendix 2: 8 LINES Of Personal Development Summary

(Through 4 Levels of Development)

Levels

1 Responder   2 Conformist   3 Individualist   4 Conscient

Lines

1 Motivation

From Non-aware, Narcissistic & Needy,   To   Doing   &   Belonging,   To Individuality,   To Something Beyond Personal Self
Notes:

2 Identity

From Self-Protective, To Conventional Roles and Rules, To Authentic, To Transpersonal
Notes:

3 Focus

From Scattered, To Intensifying Concentration, To Integrating, To Open Focus
Notes:

273

4 Relationships

<u>From Being Needy,</u>   <u>To Cooperative,</u>   <u>To Genuine,</u>   <u>To</u>
<u>Interconnected</u>
Notes:

5 Emotions

<u>From Anger, Fear, Greed & Need, To Self Control, To Recognizing And</u>
<u>Expressing Emotions, To Well-Being</u>
Notes:

6 Ethics

<u>From Getting Away With Things, To Reward & Punishment, To Personal</u>
<u>Integrity, To Universal Compassion, Justice & Service</u>
Notes:

7 Awareness

<u>From The Merely Physical & Self-Centered, To Eyes Of Mind & Heart, To Soul,</u>
<u>To Spirit And Being</u>
Notes:

8 Wisdom

<u>From Personal Boundaries Of Pain & Suffering, To Conventional Answers, To</u>
<u>Personal Meaning, To Direct Experience Of Timeless Spirit</u>
Notes:

Appendix 3: Issues Tracker

See examples below on how a life issue changes from level to level.

For your issues, in the Personal and Social boxes, list a life issue on the left, and see how it would manifest for you on life's four levels.

ISSUE	Level 1	Level 2	Level 3	Level 4
Examples	**Responder**	**Conformist**	**Individualist**	**Conscient**
Detachment	Denial	Discipline	Choice	Freedom
Independence	Willful rebel	Personally responsible group player	Self reliant self starter	Interdependent being
Love	Enmeshment	Cooperation	Respect for differences	All are one
Perfection	Rigidity	Material appearances	Uniqueness acknowledged	Universal acceptance of all as they are
Power	Control over others	Compromise	Candid diplomacy	Loving service

275

PERSONAL ISSUES	Responder	Conformist	Individualist	Conscient
Tracker				
MOTIVATION				
IDENTITY				
FOCUS				

EMOTIONS				
RELATION-SHIP				

ETHICS				
AWARENESS				
WISDOM				

Lifewheel: Your Choices at Life's Every Turn

SOCIAL ISSUES Tracker	Responder	Conformist	Individualist	Conscient
FAMILY				
POLITICS				

RELIGION/ ARTS				
SEX/ CLOSENESS				
SOCIAL SITUATIONS				

WORK				

Appendix 4: Lifewheel Mascot

Meet S Elf, the trickster mascot, who acts as companion and jokester along the way. S Elf, tends to see the big picture, is a great companion to his fellow travelers, supporting them with good humor and care.

S Elf is a companion who helps on the journey of life. He is a trickster god, bringing luck for the journey, mysterious, protective and full of mischief and sweetness. He moves adeptly and swiftly, changing perspective as needed and sometimes playing innocent to get by. He is endlessly curious, and aware of human foibles, supporting others through life's passages, gently freeing uptight, imprisoned souls, sometimes offending, but always supporting what needs to get free. S Elf sees life as the endless adventure of greater and greater self-realization.

Here is a little personal info about S Elf.

Favorite clothing line: that of an informal traveler, with an emblem slogan, "Just Be It!" The shoe may have little wings on it. He also wears a wide-brimmed hat with wings.

S Elf's body type is that of Abraham Maslow's "Hierarchy of Needs" Pyramid.

S Elf is eager to provide personal assistance to you. He eagerly awaits hearing of your dilemmas, to help you through them. Just ask S Elf.

Appendix 5: Personal & Social Development

Where are you in the spiral of life?

Personal Development

To track your progress, mark where you are in lines of personal development, with dated, explanatory notes in your Lifewheel Journal. You might also want to add your own lines of development.

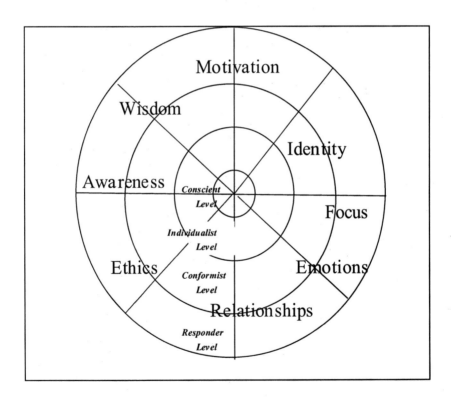

Social Domains

Mark where you are in the social domains, with dated, explanatory notes in your Lifewheel Journal, to help track your progress.

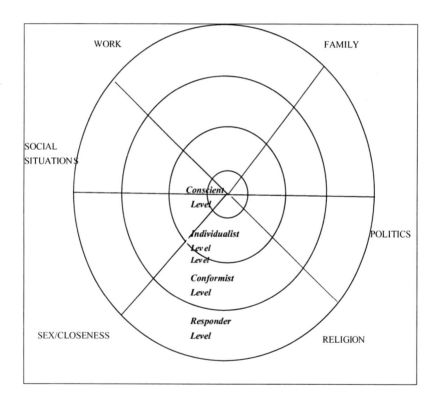

Appendix 6: Lifewheel Basic List of Recommended Readings (*Core Books)

General Overview of Integral Personal Development and Personal Practice

Deepak Chopra, How to Know God, A
James Fowler, Stages of Faith, A, C
Kathy Kouzmanoff, Lifewheel: Your Choices at Life's Every Turn, A
Abraham Maslow, The Farther Reaches of Human Nature, P
*Leonard and Murphy, The Life We are Given, H, P
Gail Sheehy, Passages; New Passages, A
Jenny Wade, Changes of Mind, P
*Ken Wilber, A Theory of Everything, A

> ➤ Books giving overviews of integral personal development or daily practices for personal change, including autobiographies and biographies

Needy, Naïve, Narcissistic and Non-Aware Responder
Level 1 Body (Non-Aware Ego/No Ego)

*Melodie Beattie, Co-Dependent No More, A, I
Alcoholics Anonymous, Big Book 4th Edition, A
Alcoholics Anonymous, Twelve Steps & Twelve Traditions, A
Christopher Lasch, The Culture of Narcissism, P
M Scott Peck, The Children of the Lie, P
M Scott Peck, The Road Less Traveled, P

> ➤ Books identifying dysfunction, denial, ineffectiveness, irresponsibility and addictions, with ways of overcoming them personally and socially

Smart, Sassy, Savvy and Successful Conformist
Level 2 Mind and Heart (Ego)
Bolles, What Color is Your Parachute?, A
*Steven Covey, Seven Habits of Highly Effective People, A P
Daniel Goleman, Emotional Intelligence, P
Daniel Goleman, Social Intelligence, P
Norman Vincent Peale, The Power of Positive Thinking, A, C
Daniel Siegel, The Mindful Brain, P
*Tieger & Barron Tieger, The Art of Speed Reading People;
also see Do What You Are; Just Your Type, P

> ➢ Books on personal success in career and relationships,
> skills in time management, group dynamics and their
> application to social institutions

Receptive, Reflective and Real Individualist
Level 3 Soul (Ego and Self)
Jean Shinoda Bolen, Gods in Everyman; Goddesses in
Everywoman, P
Joseph Campbell, The Power of Myth, A
Eugene Gendlin, Focusing; Let Your Body Interpret Your
Dreams, H, P
Carol Gilligan, In a Different Voice, P
*Daniel Goleman, The Meditative Mind, E, A
Michael Harner, The Way of the Shaman, N
*Carl Jung, Man & His Symbols, also Modern Man in Search
of a Soul; Psyche & Symbols, The Basic Writings, etc., P
Kabbalah Studies, J
Arnold Mindell, The Shaman's Path, P, N
Thomas Moore's books on soul, P, A
Anthony Storr, Solitude, P
Jeremy Taylor, Dream Work, P
* Roger Walsh, Essential Spirituality, A

> Books on dreams, journaling, symbolism, the unconscious, myth, creating ceremony, and religious practice, that is, the means of linking ego and Self, and applying these to personal consciousness, behavior, culture, relationships and society

Conscious and Connected Conscient
Level 4 Spirit (Enlightened Ego in Service of Self/No Ego)
Coleman Barks, trans, Essential Rumi; Soul of Rumi; Rumi The Book of Love, etc., M
Deepak Chopra, Quantum Healing and other writings, E, H
Ralph Waldo Emerson, The Complete Writings, A
*Aldous Huxley, The Perennial Philosophy, A
Lao Tsu, Tao Te Ching, E
Steven Mitchell, trans, The Enlightened Heart; The Enlightened Mind, A
Raymond Moody, Life After Life, H
Andrew B Newberg, M.D., Why God Won't Go Away, H
*Richardson, Four Spiritualities, P, A
Eckhart Tolle, The Power of Now, H
Helen Schucman, A Course in Miracles, C

> Books on personal, direct experience of timeless being, transcendence, states of bliss, fruits of the Spirit and enlightenment, with their expression in relationships, culture and society

<u>Abbreviation Codes for Growth Traditions:</u>
CJM: Christian/Jewish/Muslim
E: Eastern
N: Indigenous
H: Holistic Science
P: Psychosocial
A: General, all, any

Endnotes

[1] See Ken Wilber's many works in which he describes the "quadrants."

[2] Myers Briggs Typology Inventory is a widely used personality assessment showing preference in pairs of opposites. I think it is key information for making insightful, self-aware life choices.

[3] Paul D. Tieger and Barbara Barron-Tieger, Just Your Type, Little Brown and Co., 2000.

[4] Peter Tufts Richardson, Four Spiritualities: Expressions of Self, Expressions of Spirit, Davies-Black Publishing, Palo Alto, 1996

[5] Wilber has many overview books, including Eye to Eye, No Boundary, Transformations of Consciousness, Eye of Spirit and A Theory of Everything.

[6] Dr. Roger Walsh, Essential Spirituality, John Wiley & Sons, 1999

[7] Jenny Wade, Changes of Mind, State University of New York Press, 1996

[8] Dr. Roger Walsh, Essential Spirituality, John Wiley & Sons, 1999

[9] See Richardson and Tieger and Tieger above

[10] Jenny Wade, Changes of Mind, State University of New York Press, 1996

[11] See Richardson and Tieger and Tieger above

[12] Dr. Daniel Siegel, The Mindful Brain, W.W. Norton and Company, 2007 See his work for a discussion, from a neurological perspective, of our ability to be mindful.

[13] Myers Briggs Typology Inventory (MBTI) The actual MBTI shows only general development, however, not levels of development.

[14] Exodus 20:5

[15] Myers Briggs Typology Inventory (MBTI) The actual MBTI shows only general development, however, not levels of development.

[16] Myers Briggs Typology Inventory (MBTI) The actual MBTI shows only general development, however, not levels of development.

[17] Joseph Campbell, The Power of Myth with Bill Moyers, Doubleday, 1988, P. 155

[18] Myers Briggs Typology Inventory (MBTI) The actual MBTI shows only general development, however, not levels of development.

Printed in the United States
121254LV00001B/1-90/A